A TRIANGLE HAS FOUR SIDES

A TRIANGLE HAS FOUR SIDES

Phyllis Reynolds Naylor

AUGSBURG Publishing House • Minneapolis

A TRIANGLE HAS FOUR SIDES

Photos: Michael Siluk, pp. 10, 80; Strix Pix, pp. 24, 48; Jim Cronk, p. 55; Dave Anderson, p. 94.

Library of Congress Cataloging in Publication Data

Naylor, Phyllis Reynolds.
A Triangle Has Four Sides.

Summary: Thirteen short stories of young people facing such problems as shyness, pregnancy, divorce, and jealousy.
[1. Emotional problems–Fiction. 2. Christian life–Fiction. 3. Short stories] I. Title. II. Title: Triangle has 4 sides.
PZ7.N24Tr 1984 [Fic] 83-72123
ISBN 0-8066-2067-6 (pbk.)

Manufactured in the U.S.A. APH 10-6700

1 2 3 4 5 6 7 8 9 0 1 2 3 4 5 6 7 8 9

For people
who care about people

Contents

About This Book

Relationships are many-sided. They have sharp angles that hurt, and unexpected turns that delight. They give us open spaces to explore and corners where we feel closed in. We live in a maze of overlapping relationships, not only with friends, but with family, neighbors, and society.

We can move to a new address, change the way we live, even take a new name. But we can never, not even for a moment, get outside our own bodies and be someone else.

However, if we care enough to really understand what someone else is feeling, we may discover we have built a bridge and that we both are richer for it.

All to Herself Alone

Something wasn't right. Pat set the rake against the garage and took off her gloves. She had the world in her hands. But the something was always there, and she didn't know what it was.

"Pat!" Mrs. Leland called out the back door. "Joe just phoned and said he'd pick you up earlier—wants to take you out to eat. You can finish the yard tomorrow."

Pat slowly got ready. What more could she possibly want? Joe was the greatest guy she'd ever met—vice president of the senior class, track star, a member of her church, and her folks really liked him. She loved him so much it hurt.

She brushed her hair mechanically. When you were in love, birds were supposed to sing and stars shine, and they did—sometimes. But sometimes the song was sad, the stars seemed to weep, and Pat could only wonder what was the matter with her—or him—or them.

Now and then they talked of marriage, and Joe

meant every word of it. But he felt it too—this something—this thing that wasn't right. Pat could tell. And for some reason, as she dressed tonight, it haunted her even more.

"Hi, Joe." She was wearing a brown wool skirt and cream sweater, her blond hair cascading over her shoulders.

Joe rose from the couch—tall, good-looking, kind—everything a girl could want. "Ready?"

"Ready."

The car moved noiselessly down the street, across the bridge, and out Meadow Road.

"Thought we'd drive up to Marshall to eat," Joe said. "I wanted to have some time to talk."

"What did you want to talk about?"

"Let's wait till after we eat." He gave a little laugh. "I talk better on a full stomach."

They passed the barn where the church youth group rented the wagon for the fall hayrides. Pat remembered last year. She and Joe had sat together near the back of the wagon, watching the lanterns swing back and forth.

"Happy?" Joe had asked.

"Almost," she had answered.

"Only almost?"

"Oh, Joe, I love you so much I could die. But you've got so many other things going. You don't have time for me."

Joe had looked at her strangely. "Do you really want me to give up something?"

"Yes."

"What?"

"Everything but me." Her eyes were laughing but her mouth wasn't.

"Well—I guess the debate team could go. I—really enjoy it, but if something's got to give. . . ."

Now the car rounded the bend beyond the weathered barn and Pat's shoulder touched Joe's.

"What were you thinking about?" Joe asked.

She tried to smile. "I was remembering the hayride last year."

"That's a coincidence. So was I."

They turned out on the highway. On the left was the new stadium where next year's seniors would play. Pat wondered idly where she and Joe would be then. How could she bear separate colleges? She could scarcely stand an evening without him now.

The old track and football fields were more convenient, she thought to herself—only three blocks from her house. She walked over there every evening when Joe was running. She would sit on the empty bleachers, waiting patiently until his workout was over. An uncomfortable feeling swept through her again as she remembered the day Joe's team had won, making them state champions. Pat had been there with a glowing smile when Joe came in off the field, breathless and exuberant.

"Hey, girl, get lost," one of the runners had said jokingly as he passed Pat. "The team's going out for a steak dinner—courtesy of the coach."

Pat had glanced quickly at Joe, her eyes showing the hurt.

"Sort of a tradition," Joe explained.

"But Joe!" The hurt in her eyes deepened. "I—I had

a party all planned! I baked a cake and everything!"

"You didn't tell me about it."

"I wanted it to be a surprise! You've *got* to come, Joe!"

Joe turned to the runner beside him. "Hate to let her down," he said, his voice suddenly weary. "Explain it to the coach, will you?"

Pat's mind returned to the present as they turned into the restaurant parking lot. Inside, the hostess seated them at a table in the corner. After they ordered, they talked of school, church—everything, Pat realized, except themselves.

When the food arrived, Joe sat absently toying with his fork. Pat watched with a strange foreboding. Suddenly he reached across the table and put his hand on hers without looking at her. "I don't know how to say this, Pat," he began.

He didn't have to say more. His voice told her all she needed to know. "What is it, Joe?"

Still he did not look at her. "I love you, Pat. I really do. . . ."

"But?" she questioned.

He smiled uneasily. "There's always a 'but,' isn't there? I guess what I'm trying to say is that maybe love isn't enough right now."

"What do you mean?"

"I wish I knew. I've been thinking about this a long time, and I still can't put it into words."

"I know. Neither can I."

"You feel it too?"

"I just know that something isn't right. Mom says I've got such a good thing that I keep sticking pins in it to see if it will burst. But I think there's more to it than that."

"I do too."

"What do you think it is, Joe?"

"Well—you'll hate me for this—but sometimes I—I feel that wherever I go, you're there. I'm glad, but—sometimes I wish you weren't. I think we need a break for awhile—from each other. I want to be able to do the other things that are important to me without—without feeling guilty about you."

Pat withdrew her hand and stared at her plate as she nervously twisted her napkin. "If you really feel that way," she said finally, "I guess it's best to break up."

"I didn't mean we should stop seeing each other, Pat. I just want to be free to grow this year. I want to take on other responsibilities—besides you."

"You want to play the field. Is that what you're trying to say?"

"Believe me, that's the least part of it. I wasn't thinking about any other girl. I've tried to explain before—the debate team and all the rest. . . ."

Pat put down her napkin suddenly. "You're still mad about that, aren't you Joe?"

"Yes, I guess I am."

"Well, I didn't know that a couple hours debating every Tuesday night were more important than—than being with me."

"Pat, can't you understand? It isn't just the debate team, it's everything."

They sat for a few minutes without speaking. "I thought love was supposed to be sharing," Pat said finally. "I thought when you were in love, you always wanted the other person around—that you put the other person before everything else in the world."

Joe didn't answer.

"Maybe you just don't like being close, Joe."

He jerked his head up. "Pat, sometimes I feel like I'm suffocating! I don't have room to breathe—to be myself!"

Pat reached for her purse. "Well, I sure don't want to suffocate anybody," she said hotly. "We've got different ideas about love, that's all."

The drive home seemed unbearably long. Pat couldn't stand the silence and felt relieved when they came to a stop at her house.

"Pat," Joe began, "I'm sorry if anything I've said has hurt you."

"There's no need to feel sorry for me," Pat said, getting out. "You aren't so great that I'm going to wilt because you're not around."

"Pat—"

The door slammed and Pat ran inside and up the stairs to her room. The house was empty. Her parents were out for the evening and had not expected her home until late. She threw herself down on the bed and lay motionless, too hurt even to cry. Finally, she heard Joe's car start outside and drive off.

She had known it would happen. She knew he loved her, but for the whole year that she had known him, she'd never really felt she owned him.

She never owned him. Somehow it sounded strange when she thought about it—as though he were a puppy or a book or a lump of clay she could carry in her pocket.

The room suddenly seemed stifling. Pat got up and went outside. She walked slowly up and down the block, kicking along in the leaves beneath the street lights. She tried not to think about it any more, but it was there – inescapable. The whole pattern of how she had loved Joe—the way she had hovered over him, always there, always ready to take possession, always jealous of the things he did that didn't include her.

Three weeks before, at their youth group, the pastor had talked about love and marriage. "What makes a good marriage?" someone had asked. His answer had been so simple it had escaped her: "A good marriage, a good love, brings out the best in each other. Each one helps the other to be the best possible person he or she can become."

She drew in her breath sharply as she started back up the street. How much had she helped Joe become his best possible self? Any? How much had she stunted him, deprived him of the other things that were important too? In wanting him all to herself, how much had she shut him away from others?

She walked thoughtfully back into the house. It was more than just Joe. By clinging to him so tightly, she was not only driving him away, but stunting herself as well. By making Joe her whole world, no matter how much she loved him, she was shutting out the many other things that made her a complete person.

She suddenly realized the phone was ringing and she picked up the receiver.

"Pat!" The voice on the line was tender in its concern. "You've got to listen to me now. I make horrible speeches but maybe I can do better over the phone. I wasn't suggesting we never see each other again. I just don't want to go back to—to what it was before. I mean. . . ."

It was a second chance, and not every girl had one. How much did she really love Joe? Enough to let him live his own life?

"Joe," she said, "let's begin again as friends."

"I love you, Pat. It's more than friends."

"I know. But maybe if we think like friends for a while, I can learn to love you without—without trying to own you."

There was a silence.

"Can I see you tomorrow?" Joe asked.

Her heart leaped. But she hesitated. "I'd love to, but no. Let's wait until Saturday. And let's do something different. I want to make a fresh start."

"Pat, you're great!"

Like Ships in the Night

CHARACTERS: A boy, a girl, and a crowd.

TIME AND PLACE: Friday night at a high school dance.

SETTING: About 100 young people are gathered in a gymnasium. The band has just taken a break, and people are milling about on the edge of the dance floor. A few sit at tables. Enter boy on left.

BOY (to himself): *I don't know why I come to dances. Same crowd, same music, same talk. If all the girls in the world are like this, I'll never get married.*

GIRL (alone at table): *Another dull Friday night. I wonder if there are any guys in the world who talk about anything but cars and football.*

BOY: (moving aimlessly about room): *Maybe there's something wrong with me. Everybody else seems to be having a good time. Everybody else thinks the band is great. What would they say if they knew I'd spent the afternoon listening to a Vivaldi concerto?*

GIRL (noticing boy): *There's that tall boy from French class. I wonder what he's like. He always seemed so nice. Now he's talking with that blonde in the blue dress. She's a cheerleader, isn't she? Bet it's about football. She really knows how to talk to a guy.*

BOY (moving on around the room): *That girl never heard of Vivaldi, that's for sure. Hey, there's that dark-haired girl from French sitting alone. She always seemed like she might be interesting.*

GIRL: *Oh no! He's coming over here! What'll I talk about? Who did the football team play last? I can't remember.*

BOY: Hi. I'm a fellow French sufferer, remember? Saving this table for anybody?

GIRL (smiling): No. Sit down.

BOY: *I don't suppose I'm lucky enough to find out she came alone. Probably came with a bunch of rah-rah girl friends.*

Did you come by yourself tonight?

GIRL: *If I tell him the truth he'll think I'm a creep.*

No. I came with some of my girl friends.

BOY: *Just what I thought. Still, she may have heard of Vivaldi.*

Well, what do you do with your time when you aren't studying French idioms?

GIRL: *I wonder what he'd say if I told him I play the flute and do oil painting. No, I'd better go slow or I'll never see him again.*

Oh, this and that. What about yourself?

BOY: *This and that! What does she mean? Watch TV probably.* Well, I. . . . *No. If I tell her about listening to Vivaldi all afternoon she'll laugh me right out of the room.* Oh, I listen to records. (Laughs uneasily) File my nails, wash my socks.

GIRL: *What kind of guy is this, anyway? At least he has a sense of humor. Maybe I should tell him about oil painting after all.*

Do you ever . . . uh . . . go to museums . . . ?

BOY: *She's got me pegged, all right. Look how she's staring at me. I better wise up before she walks right out on me.*

Depends on whom I'm with.

GIRL: *Now what did he mean by that? I'll bet he's comparing me with the blonde. What he's really saying is that if he took her out, they'd really live. If he took me out, I'm so dull we'd end up in a museum.*

Well, I don't go much either.

That's a lie. What did you think of the game last Saturday?

BOY: *I knew it, she's just like all the rest. If I told her about Vivaldi she'd think he was a halfback.*

It was really great, wasn't it?

How do I know? I wasn't even there.

GIRL: *See? That's what he wanted to talk about all the time. If I'm ever going to attract a nice guy like him, I've just got to learn to talk about things that interest him. And to think I almost ruined it by telling him about the show at the art museum!*

The big game's next Saturday, though – over in Logansville. If we beat them, we're really in! *There, that sounded better. But how I hate it!*

BOY: Yeah. I guess everybody will be going to that game.
Everybody but me. I've got two tickets to a play, and I can't find one sane girl to ask to go with me.

GIRL: *If I play it right, maybe he'll ask me to go to the game with him. It's too bad, though. There are a hundred things I'd rather do. What would happen if I told him I like to walk in the rain?*

Do you ever like to walk in the rain?
Oh, my word! Now I've done it.

BOY (looking up suddenly): What?
Say, maybe she is interesting after all.

GIRL (flushing): I mean . . . I . . . uh . . . I . . . have a girl friend who likes to do that. She . . . oh . . . always was sort of a nut.

BOY: *It was too good to be true. She's just like all the rest. Boys, clothes, and cars. If I ever find a girl with an ounce of individuality, I'd date her so fast it would make her head spin.*

Well, I see some guys I know over there, so guess I'll shove off. Don't let the French get you down. Ha ha. *Brother, I can't even stand myself. Talk about a stupid finish.*

GIRL: I won't. So long. *Now I've done it. Oh, why am I such a square! It was that bit about walking in the rain. He knew it was me all along and took off like a wet cat. Why can't I be like the blonde in the blue dress? She knows just what to say to a guy. Now he'll never ask me out.*

I'm sure glad I didn't tell him about the art show. He'd blab it all over school! Still . . . I don't want to be just like everyone else. Isn't there anyone around like me?

BOY: *And to think I almost asked her to that play! She probably would have wanted popcorn all through it, for Pete's sake. And she looked so nice.*

I always thought I'd like to know her better, but now I'm sorry. She's as shallow as the rest of them. Maybe worse. Guess I'll go to the play with my cousin.

A Triangle Has Four Sides

Larry Bressler shoved his plate away and stared apathetically into the mirror behind the counter.

"You want anything else?" the woman in the uniform asked.

Larry shook his head, and she turned back to the grill.

A classmate plunked down on the stool next to him. "I see you're eating out," he said, opening the menu. "This must be the week your folks went to Florida. Boy, your dad's got it made. Sales conference in Miami every winter. Too bad they can't put you on the expense account too, huh?"

Larry tried to smile.

"Why don't you come over and stay with me?" the boy continued. "At least you'd have home cooking."

Larry fumbled in his pocket for change. "Thanks, Chuck, but I just stopped to get a sandwich on my way home from the library. Mom's home."

"She didn't go along this year, huh?"

"No." Larry stood up. "Well, got to get working on my history paper. See you around."

"Right. Take it easy."

He knew, Larry decided as he made his way to the cashier. *Everybody knew.* Everybody knew that a pretty brunette named Evelyn was accompanying dad to Florida this year and that the Bressler marriage was finished. The anger inside him was so great he could hardly breathe.

"Larry?"

He closed the door and threw his coat on a chair. "Yeah?"

A thin-faced woman came out of the kitchen. "Did you have lunch?"

"Yeah. I got a sandwich downtown."

Mrs. Bressler reached for the coat, frowning. "Why didn't you call? I had lunch all made for you."

"It's okay. I'll eat it for supper."

Larry went up to his room and spread his notebooks out on his desk. The phone rang and his mother answered it in the hall below.

Larry sat listening. Strange how sharp and shrill her voice was. Had it always been this way, or just since dad left on this trip? He still remembered how it sounded the morning dad went to the airport.

"Business is business," he'd heard his father say. "Evelyn is a member of the firm. She has as much right to go as anyone. . . ."

Mrs. Bressler's shrill laugh had cut him off. "*Business!* Do you really think I believe that? Do you think I've been blind and deaf all these months—that there's one person in town who doesn't know what's going on?"

"All right, Betty, stop it! You could have come if you'd wanted to."

"And be humiliated?" Larry's mother had screamed. "Sit there as your wife, when. . . ."

Now, as Larry tried to organize his term paper, the same shrill voice came zigzagging up the stairs. Mrs. Bressler was talking to her sister:

"He said we'd talk about it when he got back. He thinks that's all there is to it—after 17 years. Well, he's in for a surprise, because I'm not giving him a divorce. I don't care what he does. He can move in with her, as far as I care. But I'm keeping the house, and I'm keeping him tied. . . ."

Larry's blood ran cold. He sprang up suddenly and slammed his door as hard as he could, rattling the windows and knocking the calendar off the wall. Then he sat down helplessly on the edge of the bed, soft choking noises in his throat.

A few moments later his mother opened the door.

"What in the world, Larry!" she scolded tensely. "Just what was that all about?"

"What do you care?" Larry cried savagely. "You take your revenge. I'll take mine. . . ."

He expected a blowup when his father came home from Florida, but there was none. At first there was icy silence between his parents. Each morning Mr. Bressler rose first, made his coffee, and left the house. Each evening he came home long after dinner was over. On weekends, he came to the table as usual, ate silently, or asked Larry superficial questions about school. Some nights, and some weekends, he didn't come home at all.

Larry couldn't stand the way things went on with no resolution. Maybe dad wasn't going to ask for a divorce so mom couldn't have the satisfaction of saying no. Maybe he'd already asked. Maybe he was sticking it out for Larry's sake. Maybe. . . .

He grew sullen with his mother, surly with his father. At dinner one evening, when his father asked his grade on an algebra test, Larry snapped, "I don't want to answer any more questions, if you don't mind. I'm tired of carrying on a monolog. Find somebody else to talk to. You don't seem to have any trouble making friends."

Mr. Bressler stared at his son intently without speaking. Then he silently picked up his fork again. The cups and spoons clinked against the table. Mrs. Bressler's voice, syrupy and smug, came from the other end of the table:

"Larry, how about you and I driving into Bradford Saturday night? We could eat out at a restaurant there, and. . . ."

"No," Larry said through clenched teeth. "I'm not interested in being your escort, either. Don't expect me to fill in the gaps."

Mr. Bressler stopped going to church. Larry went with his mother, but he always found an excuse to sit with someone else. Finally he went to see the minister one evening after school.

"Dad's loused everything up—for all of us," Larry said in the pastor's office. "Sometimes I hate him for the way he's having an affair in—in public, practically. And yet, I think I hated him even more when it was secret. I feel like I hate Mom, too. I don't know why.

I just wish she was different—warmer, I guess. And I suppose Dad does too. I guess that's what's wrong."

"It's hard to tell, Larry," Pastor James said. "It's a tough situation, and it's hurting several people, but none of us knows the whole story."

Larry sat bitterly drumming his fingers on the arm of the chair. "They only think about themselves. Dad, mom, Evelyn . . . what do they care how I feel? They think a triangle only has three sides. They're wrong—it has four. They're all on a sinking boat and they'll pull me down with them."

"That's one place you're wrong, Larry," the pastor said earnestly. "It's your life, and nobody can really ruin it but you. They can give you a rough time, it's true, but there's no reason your life has to turn out the same way unless you let it."

Larry walked home thoughtfully in the January cold. He'd been noticing a lot of things since the affair began almost a year ago. Little things that had gone on as long as he could remember—things he'd taken for granted the way you do when you live with somebody. He'd noticed how mom never waited with dinner if dad was late, no matter what the reason. She'd clear off the dishes promptly at 6:30 and dad would have to fix his own supper when he got home. He'd noticed the way mom always went to bed early, leaving dad to watch television or read alone. He noticed the way they forgot each other's birthdays — except perhaps for a joking remark at the table, and anniversaries weren't mentioned at all. It wasn't exactly the kind of home where husband and wife enjoyed each other, and he wondered if they ever had.

He had a double date on Friday night. Chuck Evans had talked him into it.

"I don't care what your dad does, Larry, you can't be a hermit," Chuck said. "Come on. I've got it all set up with Sara and Chrissy."

They took the girls bowling and then out to eat.

"I'm really hungry," Chuck said, "What say we drive out to the Point for a burger or something?"

In the back seat, Sara leaned her head on Larry's arm. "I really had fun tonight," she said.

Larry smiled down at her and realized he felt good for the first time in months. "I should have asked you out sooner."

Sara's eyes twinkled. "Yes," she said, "you should have."

The Point was a favorite spot. It was quiet that evening, and they took a table near the back. They had just sat down when Larry's eye caught the man at the table behind him. He turned to see his father, his arm around Evelyn, talking intimately.

Mr. Bressler looked up. Flushing, he took in the situation at a glance, waved a brief hello to Larry with two fingers and reached for his check. Larry sat like stone, neither returning the wave nor speaking. The brunette woman picked up her purse and went out quickly through a side entrance, followed by Larry's father.

At four in the morning, Larry was still awake, staring at the pattern of light and dark on his ceiling. Earlier, he had heard his mother sobbing in her room. Finally she had gone to sleep. But Larry's eyes would not close.

At five, he got up, packed some things in his bag, took what money he had from his dresser, and crept outside. His father's car was still gone. He took a bus downtown and then the first Greyhound leaving the station. A few miles out of town, on impulse, he got off the bus and walked a half mile back to a motel. He rented a room and lay down on the bed, feeling sick to his stomach.

He didn't know why he had left or what he hoped would happen. All he knew was that something had to give. He fell asleep and slept for several hours. When he woke up, he went to the motel restaurant for eggs and toast. Afterward, he bought a magazine and took it to his room.

By noon there wasn't anything left to do. Mom would have missed him by now—dad, too. He lay on his back all afternoon, thinking.

Before dinner that evening, he listened to the news broadcast but there was no mention of his name. He went to bed early.

When he woke Sunday morning, he felt rested for the first time in months. Far away, a dog barked. A truck roared past the motel and then another. In the quiet of their aftermath, Larry could hear a church bell pealing out across the frozen fields.

He got up slowly, dressed, and went to the restaurant for breakfast. He was anonymous in the dining room. No one knew his name or his problems. He realized suddenly how completely individual he was. He could run his life the way he wished. Dad and mom had attempted to solve their problem by running away. Dad looked for love somewhere else. Mom retreated into a vindictive little shell, where she shut out the world and her husband both. And Larry. . . .

He pushed away his eggs and looked out over the surrounding fields. For a while, he had almost been trapped in the pattern. He, too, had run for the nearest exit. But someone had to break the chain. . . .

He walked to his room and packed his bag. He had given his parents a scare, but it was not really going to change a thing. In fact – and he realized it now for the first time – there was nothing he could do to solve their problem. But he was going back. He could not fill the gap in his mother's life that dad had left, and he would have to help her see that. And he wasn't going to drive his dad even further away by digs and snide remarks. If he met dad in public with Evelyn, he wouldn't run from it. Let dad and Evelyn do the running and excusing. He would take his parents as they were, with prayers for them both. But he was responsible for one person, and as long as he lived his own life well, he would hold his head high.

In Spite of Spite

On Good Friday, she awoke feeling furious. For several hours the night before she had lain there thinking up ways of revenge, playing them out in her mind. And when she opened her eyes to rain on an already somber day, the fury welled up again inside her, and she sloshed off to school, full of silent rage.

There were a thousand novels about plain, undistinguished girls who found romance and happiness. But did anybody write about the frustrations of an attractive, talented girl? Ordinary girls could laugh and say something about, "a plain girl like me," and nobody would care. But what could a beautiful girl say when she wasn't allowed to use her creative abilities?

Elaine plowed through the puddles in her high boots, not caring about the mud that splashed up on her poncho. She was fed up with being treated like a show-off every time she tried to do something well.

Two months before, she had been given the soprano solo in one of the numbers the youth choir was performing on Easter Sunday. This Easter, youth choirs from all over the city were coming together for a festival of music in Fulton Park. Each would perform several numbers for the thousands of people who would gather there on the hillside.

On Thursday night, however, Mrs. Richards had announced that each choir was limited to 15 minutes. "We have to eliminate one of our numbers," she told the choir regretfully. "You've all worked so hard on all the anthems. I feel bad about dropping any at all, so I'm leaving the choice up to you."

Even before she heard the first whisper, Elaine knew which anthem would be cut. Even before she saw Lisa and Mary exchange glances, she knew the verdict. It came as no surprise when Lisa said innocently, "What about the number by Handel?"

Mrs. Richards looked quickly around the group. "Oh, dear, that's the one with Elaine's solo. What do the rest of you think?"

"We never did do it very well," Mary added. "The other anthems are better."

"Well," Mrs. Richards said, "If you're all agreed, then. . . ." She turned to Elaine. "Do you mind too much, dear?"

"Of course not," Elaine had lied.

But she did. She had spent hours rehearsing it. And why shouldn't she have been given the solo? What was she supposed to do—go drown herself because she could sing? Pretend she couldn't? Would it really have made sense to give the solo to Lisa or Mary, who couldn't even reach high D?

Moodily she reached her locker and fumbled with

the combination. There was no one she could talk to about it – not even her parents. When she tried to discuss her problems with mother – the envy of the other girls, the petty jealousies, the snide remarks– her mother always listened patiently and said always, always, always "I know it's hard, Elaine, but look at you. You have so much, and some girls have so little. You can afford to be humble. You'll just have to be as sweet and kind and unselfish as possible."

Well, she was sick and tried of being sweet and kind. If anybody thought she didn't have problems, they just didn't know her. Girls resented her–because they were afraid she was going to take away their boyfriends – so there were only three girls at school she considered real friends. And when Elaine got the lead role in the senior play, one of those girls became so jealous that now there were only two left. Though she usually had plenty of dates, many of the boys she would like to have known better never asked her out. They assumed she was so popular she wouldn't have time.

But when Elaine had tried to explain all this to her mother, Mrs. Kelly just shook her head and said, "You have the moon. Don't ask for the stars as well."

The question was what to do now. If it had been a rational decision to cut her solo, Elaine would have accepted it. But it was as plain as the sun in the sky that the anthem was cut out of spite. If she'd had a solo part in one of the other anthems instead, the girls would have voted to cut that one. Should she really continue being the sweet-voiced Elaine, always humble, always unselfish, and allow them to walk all over her year after year? Or should she finally assert her right to be treated like a human being?

She thought about it all through history and English. All she had to do was stay home on Easter morning, claiming a sore throat, and the choir would regret what they'd done. At least two of the remaining anthems had difficult soprano parts, and if Elaine wasn't there to lead them, Mary, Lisa, and the other sopranos would fold up. Mary didn't even try the high notes. She just opened her mouth and faked it. Why not stay home and let them suffer the consequences? Christ never said you had to be a doormat to be Christian.

Elaine decided she would give them no hint of what she planned to do. When she met Mary and Lisa in the gym class, she breezed cheerfully by, did her sit-ups vigorously, hit the volleyball with enthusiasm, and bounced on down to the showers.

She stayed a long time in one of the back stalls as the hot water soothed her, and was about to step out when she heard Mary's voice in another row, saying to Lisa, "I'll bet she cried her eyes out last night—big Easter star with no place to shine."

"Probably won't show up Sunday. That's my guess," Lisa ventured.

Elaine waited until they had left before she dressed. She wouldn't give them the satisfaction of being right. But now she was trapped. She couldn't even get revenge. She either had to play the childish temperamental prima donna, making the whole choir feel guilty and uncomfortable because of the actions of a few, or she had to accept all the rottenness others dumped on her, never showing her feelings. She hated herself and the others and the world and Easter and everything that made her life so complicated.

Elaine sulked all day Saturday. She could see her life stretching before her as one big hassle. There would always be enemies looking for flaws in what they *thought* was an all-too-perfect girl. They would despise her successes, gloat over her failures, rejoice in any misfortunes she suffered as though she had them coming. If she was assertive, they would hate her. If she continued to cater to them, being overly sweet and humble, she would hate herself, and they would laugh at her behind her back. What was the alternative? Or was there any? *Dear God,* she prayed that evening, *if there is an answer, help me find it.*

Sunday dawned just as an Easter morning should—soft with dew, glowing with warmth, with streaks of red and yellow brightening the sky. People were coming from all over the city to hear the music—elderly people from nursing homes, children from the psychiatric hospital, prisoners from the county jail. People with many needs and many different types of problems were coming to revitalize their lives with the beauty of music. Could it do the same for her?

Elaine sat on the edge of her bed and brushed her hair. The rising sun made a latticework design on her wall, and a young mockingbird tried a new song outside her window. *Easter,* she thought, *a day to commemorate the man who said of his enemies, "Father, forgive them, for they do not know what they are doing."*

Couldn't she, for such a little thing, also forgive

hers—even if they knew very well what they were doing? Even when she knew they would do it again?

The answer, Elaine realized suddenly, was larger than Mary and Lisa—larger than herself. It didn't lie in groveling before those who envied her. It didn't mean aggressively forging ahead. The only answer was to live her life as well as she could, as kindly and generously and thoughtfully as she could, and then not worry about it. There would be other problems, other people, other jealousies, and she would have to make sure that in using her own talents, she never stepped on others. But beyond that, she would let the matter rest.

As for today, she would sing as best she could for the lonely, the sick, the disappointed, the frightened—the thousands who were coming to celebrate the meaning of Easter. She would greet Mary and Lisa and all the others cordially, with no bitterness. She would refuse to let a grudge dwell any longer in her heart. If there was pettiness and childish revenge, it would have to come from Mary and Lisa, not from her. She would set her sights on the promise of Easter and hope the others would do the same.

"Make a joyful noise unto the Lord," rang out the minister's voice to the throngs on the hillside.

And joyously, Elaine lifted her voice in song.

One of the Gang

"Bill, I wish you wouldn't shout at me."

"I'm *not* shouting! I'm simply stating facts!"

Bill Evans took a deep breath and tried to keep his voice under control. He and mom had known this was coming for a long time, and now that things were out in the open, he felt both guilty and relieved.

"You're just prejudiced," he continued. "You think that anybody associated with motorcycles is automatically low and cheap. It's good experience for me to get out and mingle with people of different backgrounds. It doesn't mean I'm going to be like them." He was annoyed at the way in which his mother vigorously swished the dishcloth in the pan. That, and the two spots of color in her cheeks, meant she was upset.

"It isn't that, Bill. I don't want you to be a—a snob, but you have to think of your future, too. I'm sure that anyone who knows you respects you, but what about those who don't know you? What about the people who simply remember they saw you racing around town on a motorcycle? After all, you're going to be looking for a job this summer, and you don't want to ruin your chances. Motorcycles aren't necessarily bad, but why did you pick the boys from the east end to run around with? You know their reputations. . . ."

"What in the world are you two arguing about?" The kitchen door swung open, and Julie came in. "I could hear you clear out on the back porch."

Bill smiled faintly at his younger sister. No other guy in the whole state of Indiana was as devoted to a kid sister as Bill was. When his father had died five years before, Bill was left the "man of the house" as far as raising Julie was concerned. But Julie herself was no drip. She was smart and always saw eye to eye with him.

"Oh, nothing much," Bill said aloud, giving her hair a tweak. "Mom thinks I'm going to be influenced by the Racers—taint my solid gold personality or something."

"Oh, Mom, don't be ridiculous! They may be a little rowdy, but they're loads of fun!" Julie opened the refrigerator door and rummaged around. "Specially Dan! He's cute."

Mrs. Evans dumped the pan of dishwater in the sink, and Bill heard her murmur. "Maybe the Racers can't influence you, Bill, but they're certainly influencing somebody else."

Oh, nuts, Bill thought as he went upstairs to put on his heavy boots. *Julie just thinks they're cute and funny. She's not silly enough to let herself get carried away. That's what I'm here for, and I'd never let that happen. So what's Mom got to worry about?*

The noise of motorcycles outside grew louder, and with a roar that sounded like they were tearing into the living room they turned up the driveway and came to a shuddering halt by the garage.

Someone gave an ear-splitting whistle through his fingers and followed it with a long, low wolf whistle, intended, probably, for Julie.

Julie was sitting on the back porch railing when Bill came down, swinging her legs over one side and giggling at the antics of the crowd in the driveway.

"Isn't Dan the craziest!" she said when she noticed Bill.

Bill sauntered down the back steps.

"Hi, Billy boy!" Dan gave him a slap on the back as he passed. In answer Bill leaped on his motorcycle and started it with a thunderous roar.

"Man, he's got it bad!" said Cory, laughing. "He really wants to fly."

But nobody else was in a hurry. Todd Winters had a dual set of mirrors on his cycle, and everybody had to admire them.

Then Steve said, "Hey, Julie! C'mere."

Julie flushed excitedly, but didn't move.

"What for?"

"C'mere, and I'll tell ya."

"Tell me up here."

"Come on. I want to give you a ride."

He didn't know why, but Bill was surprised to see Julie jump off the railing and walk toward Steve.

"How do I get on?" Julie asked innocently, and

somebody picked her up and set her on the seat behind Steve.

"Hey, you guys, she doesn't know how to ride," Bill said.

Steve started the motorcycle with a roar and tore out of the driveway, swaying this way and that, with Julie shrieking behind him.

"You know, that kid's growing up!" Dan said as he leered across at Bill. "She got herself a guy yet?"

"Oh, I suppose she's got a lot of boyfriends at school. I never noticed," Bill said nonchalantly.

"Well, *I* sure noticed!" Dan said. "How old is she?"

"Thirteen."

"She acts like she's 15. Real cool for her age . . . you know?"

"Don't get any ideas."

Dan laughed. "Too late for preachin', Billy boy. I already got 'em."

Bill was relieved to see Steve's motorcycle come around the corner again, and a few minutes later it thundered up the driveway. Julie got off, a little shaken, but laughing.

"That was *fast!*" she exclaimed admiringly.

"Julie!" Mrs. Evans called from the window. "I want you to come in."

Julie made a face toward the boys and went inside. They all laughed.

"Let's cruise for awhile," Cory said. "The race is on Saturday, and we gotta get ready." At a signal from Dan they went racing out of the driveway.

On Saturday Bill finished cutting the grass and put the lawnmower back in the garage. When he went into the house to wash up, Mrs. Evans and Julie were cutting out a pattern on the kitchen table. Mom looked up and smiled, and Bill knew she was making an extra special effort to be kind since they'd had it out the week before. But the problem was still there and growing bigger, and nothing short of dumping the whole crowd could possibly satisfy mom. Nevertheless, her smile reassured him, and he felt cheerful for the first time all week. And then she said something that ruined everything. "Were you planning to take the car to the lock-in tonight?"

Bill stood staring at the bar of soap in his hand: "*What* lock-in?"

"The one at church . . . that your youth group is giving. I thought you told Julie you'd take her and introduce her to everyone, since she'll be old enough to belong next year."

"Oh, I'm sorry!" Bill gasped, turning to Julie. "I completely forgot! But tonight's the race against the Sergeants." He glanced at his mother and added hurriedly: "Oh, it's okay. It's down on the old river road, and the police have blocked it off for us."

"But . . . you mean you're not going to the lock-in at all?"

"Well, I can't be two places at once, can I? We've been working up to this race for months! I'll call Dave and ask him to take Julie. He's president, and he's always looking for new kids to join the group."

"I don't want to go without you," Julie said. "It's not that important. I'll go over to Nancy's or something."

Mrs. Evans didn't answer. She got up and walked stiffly from the room, and Bill knew she was angry. Sometimes he wished she'd come right out and blow, but today he was glad she didn't. He didn't feel like having another scene with her.

After supper he went out to the garage to shine up the motorcycle. The cool night air and the starry sky seemed just right for a race.

Julie came out, her long hair trailing down her back. She was wearing a new pair of jeans and a sweater that matched her hair, and she looked more grown up and prettier than Bill had ever seen her.

"Good luck," she said. "Hope you beat the hell out of the Sergeants."

Bill stared at her. "Where'd you pick that up? You don't swear."

"Well, you guys do all the time."

"That's different . . . I don't want you talking like that."

Julie simply laughed and went on. "I'm going over to Nancy's. See you later."

After Julie left Bill realized that he was starting to take his substitute parent role more seriously. And he wasn't quite ready for Julie's new-found independence.

At that moment a pack of motorcycles thundered up the driveway and came to a screeching halt by the garage.

"Hey, man, just one hour 'til the race, and we're really hot tonight!" Cory said, patting his motorcycle fondly.

"Yeah, and I heard one of the Sergeants had brake trouble," said Dan. "Ought to be good for a score or two against 'em."

They all practiced starting and stopping in unison. A window slammed down in the house next door, but no one paid any attention. Tonight was it—the hottest race of the year!

Suddenly Dan gave a low whistle. "Hey, she looks *great* tonight!"

Bill looked up and saw Julie walking toward them.

"I thought you went to Nancy's," he said.

"I did, but she wasn't home." Julie gave the boys a big smile.

"Lucky for us," said Steve. "Hey, you want to take another spin before we roll?"

"Leave her alone," Bill said.

"Give us a break! What are we gonna do for the next hour?" Todd groaned.

"C'mon, I'll toss you a few," someone else said, and began throwing a football around at the lower end of the driveway. "Wanna play, Bill?"

"Nah. Want to get this seat adjusted," Bill said and went into the house to get a wrench.

The group at the end of the drive was laughing loudly at a joke Steve had just told, and knowing Steve's train of thought, Bill felt he hadn't missed much. For a half hour he jiggled his seat and mirror and handlebars, and when he was sure they were perfect he stood up and wiped one arm across his face. Then he realized he hadn't seen Julie for awhile. He walked down to the end of the driveway.

"Hey, you guys seen Julie?"

"Sure," Steve grinned. "What do you think we look at when we come over here?"

"Knock it off, Steve. Where'd she go?"

"Find Dan, and you'll find her. They went walking back of the garage last I saw them," Todd said.

For the first time since he'd met the group Bill felt a surge of real dislike for the leering faces in front of him. He turned sharply and walked out to the backyard. The lawn chairs were empty, and the old stone wall at the end of the property was deserted, too. He checked the back steps, but no one was there.

He felt a slight nausea in his stomach. It wasn't like Julie to go walking off with a guy like this. He'd always thought Dan just amused her, but now he wasn't sure. He thought over some things she'd said about him, and the more he remembered, the more unsure he became.

He went out past the garage again, and this time he heard voices inside. He whirled around and ran his hand along the side until he found the door handle. He pushed open the door and snapped on the light.

Julie, her long hair disheveled, was leaning against the wall and Dan had his arms around her waist.

Julie looked scared, and she laughed nervously, but Dan turned around without letting her go and grinned at Bill.

"Hey, Billy boy, cut the light, would you?"

"Get out," Bill said hoarsely, wondering if the awful voice he heard was his own and dimly aware of the other guys crowding around the door outside.

Dan dropped his hands and stared at Bill, and

Julie walked over to her brother, embarrassed, quickly smoothing her hair again.

"Hey, man, you're really hyper about this, aren't you?" Dan said with a wondering look.

"I said get out," Bill repeated.

Dan walked slowly to the door, his eyes on Bill. To the gang outside he said, "Billy boy got scared and blew his top."

Bill followed Dan to the door.

"The race starts in 15 minutes, so you guys better go. I promised Julie I'd take her to a lock-in tonight, so I'm not going."

Steve's mouth dropped open.

"You're crazy, man! Don't let Dan bug you. He just gets carried away sometimes, that's all."

"I'm not going," Bill said firmly. "You don't need it in writing, do you?"

Nobody spoke for a moment. Then Todd said: "Come on. Billy boy's got his dander up. If we stick around long enough we might even get a sermon."

There was a loud roar as the motorcycles started up. For a minute the boys sat waiting in the driveway, thinking Bill might change his mind. Then they stepped on the gas and went tearing out the driveway and on down the street.

"You'd better go in and straighten up," Bill said, smiling at Julie so she would know he wasn't going to ask for an explanation. And the delighted look in her eyes told him she'd been counting on the lock-in more than he ever knew.

"She'll be okay," Bill murmured to himself as Julie raced up the back steps. "I'll see to that."

Promises, Promises

"Brad Fisher is *everything* a boy should be! He's tall, handsome, a basketball player, class treasurer—and he's such a neat guy."

That was Barb talking. She was so excited that she hadn't even touched her hot fudge sundae yet.

"So what else is new?" remarked Carol. "You didn't have to rush me over here right after school to tell me that."

"You want to know what else is new, Carol?" burbled Nancy excitedly, "Brad Fischer is going to ask you to the senior picnic, that's what!"

"Me!" gasped Carol.

"But don't tell *anybody,*" Paula continued. "No one's supposed to know yet."

"How could I tell anyone? He hasn't even asked me!"

"Well, he's going to." Nancy savored a spoonful of butterscotch sauce in her mouth. "He told his sister he was and she told Karen in typing class and Karen told me. He's going to call you tonight."

Carol's face went red and then white. Why, that

was about the best thing that could happen to a girl at West High. To go out with Brad Fisher, even for just one date, was every girl's dream.

"I'm so jealous I can't believe it," said Barb. "I always thought he liked you, the way he looks at you in art class. What are you going to wear?"

Carol swallowed hard. "I . . . I'm not going with Brad. I'm going with Charlie Johnson."

Three pairs of eyes stared at her in disbelief, and Paula's spoon dropped to the table top with a clank.

"Not *going* with him!" Nancy gasped, as if the sky were falling down. "I think I'm going to faint."

"*Why?*" demanded Barb. "Why on earth are you going with that creep Charlie? Of *all* the people to pick, you pick a nerd like him when you've got Mr. Wonderful at your fingertips!"

"Because Charlie asked me yesterday and I said I'd go with him," Carol explained, trying to hide her misery.

Paula looked at her like she was a two-headed monster or something. "You must be out of your mind! Call Charlie and tell him you're going with Brad! There are lots of other girls he can ask."

"This is your big chance, Carol! Don't blow it! Brad probably won't ever ask you out again if you turn him down."

"He'll think you're crazy!" Barbara concluded. "If he decides you like *Charlie* better than him, you've had it!"

"Well," Carol said numbly, "I'm not going back on my promise."

The party broke up quickly and Carol walked

moodily home by herself. If *only* Brad had called one day earlier! But he hadn't, and now she was stuck with Charlie. She wished with all her heart that something would happen and Charlie would call and say he couldn't go. Deep down she felt angry—angry at Charlie for asking her in the first place, angry at Brad for not asking earlier, angry at the girls for being so misunderstanding, and angry at herself even though she didn't know why.

Oh, there were a million excuses she could give Charlie if she called and said she couldn't go. But how could she turn around and go as Brad's date? No, she wouldn't do that to anybody.

Carol hardly ate supper and then went to her room and sat staring at the extension phone out in the hall. And then it rang. She sat frozen to the desk where she had opened her physics book. She heard her father answer.

"Carol! Telephone!"

"Coming."

With shaking knees she went out in the hall and lifted the receiver. "Hello?" She heard her father hang up downstairs.

"Hi, Carol. This is Brad Fisher. How are you?"

"Oh, hi, Brad! Just in the middle of an amps and volts assignment." She was amazed at her calmness.

"Oh, *that!* I've got a brother at the Technology Institute and he helped me a little on it. Say, Carol, you want to go with me to the senior picnic next week?"

"Oh, Brad, I'd really like to, but I was already asked. I'm really sorry."

There was a silence that seemed like eternity, and then Brad said. ". . . Oh . . . well, maybe some other time."

Carol hung up and burst into tears. Some other time! She knew there wouldn't be any other time.

The next week at school seemed to drag on endlessly. Brad was as polite as ever, but he asked Sue Carlson to go to the picnic. With Sue's good looks, red hair, and beautiful clothes, they would certainly make a handsome pair.

Charlie, too, was as polite as ever, and Carol made up her mind that regardless of what happened, she was going to be the best date she could be for that picnic. No sulking and no brooding.

Finally the day of the picnic arrived. Only seniors got the day off from school, and everybody knew they were going to have a great time. They arrived at the park early in the morning and spent the whole day boating, playing games, eating, and laughing. And they couldn't have asked for more gorgeous weather.

Charlie beamed all the way there, and Carol noticed he'd washed and shined his car especially for her. She was glad she hadn't let him down.

"We're going to have a great time," she said brightly. Charlie grinned.

The park was teeming with seniors. Already one group had an old houseboat just off shore.

"Play tennis?" Charlie asked as he parked the car.

"Not very well."

"Then I'll teach you," he grinned. "Volleyball?"

"N . . . not very well, either."

"Then I'll teach you that too. What *can* you do?"

"Well, I can wade up to my knees."

They both laughed.

"Okay," Charlie said. "You win. We'll go out to the boat first."

A minute later they had waded out to the boat and were climbing up the side. Paula, Barb, and Nancy were there with their dates, and although they smiled warmly at Charlie, Barb gave Carol a look that meant she had ruined all future chances for dates and boy friends and marriage and happiness and everything else simply by dating Charlie Johnson.

And then Carol saw them – a redheaded girl in a white sun dress and a tall, slim boy with dark hair coming across the sand. The girl walked with the calm assurance that everything wonderful belonged to her–including Brad Fisher.

All the girls on the houseboat began cooing at once and exclaiming over Sue's dress. Carol turned around and concentrated on Charlie, or rather on a snail that Charlie had found on the railing and put on her shoulder.

"Hi, Carol."

Carol turned and faced Brad as he and Sue walked across the deck.

"Hi, Brad. Hi there, Sue. Turned out to be a great day, didn't it?"

"Just what we ordered," Brad grinned. "When the senior officers plan something we always order good weather to go along with it."

"You bet!" laughed Charlie.

A group of girls came up just then, and Brad was lost in the crowd.

"Let's row out to the sandbar," Charlie suggested, so they did. They looked for frogs, collected shells, and ducked Mr. Harrison, the chemistry teacher, when he rowed out to see what was going on.

At noon everyone stuffed themselves with barbecued hamburgers, potato chips, ice cream, and still more ice cream.

In the afternoon Charlie coached Carol in tennis. Then there was a baseball game, and soon it was time for supper.

It had been a wonderful day, and Charlie turned out to be a great date. He didn't talk continually like some of the other guys, but when he did open his mouth it was usually worth listening to. He had a dry sense of humor that kept everyone in stitches, and more than one girl sat up and took notice of the tall, thin "nerd" who could tell more interesting things about more interesting subjects than all the boys in the senior class put together. But Carol didn't want to compare him with Brad. They were both wonderful in their own way.

Charlie had gone to help gather firewood and Carol was sitting on the old board fence watching the canoes come in off the river when someone touched her arm. It was Brad.

"Hey, remember me?"

"Of course I remember you," Carol laughed. "Having a good time?"

"Well . . . sure. Everyone is, I guess." He looked at her closely. "Are you?"

"Well . . . sure. Everyone is, I guess."

They laughed.

GRAND

"Listen, Carol," Brad said. "Our church group is having a cookout in a couple of weeks. Would you like to go with me? And don't say Charlie Johnson has booked every night this month. . . ."

Carol smiled. "No, he hasn't. And I'd love to go with you."

"Great!" He stood with his hands in his pockets, grinning at her. "You know, I was . . . well, not mad when you told me you were going with someone else . . . just surprised, I guess." He laughed self-consciously. "Anyway, Charlie's a nice guy–I'll say that for him."

Someone had the fire going and Sue waved to Brad.

"I'll call you next week and let you know more about the cookout," Brad said as he started to walk away. "And save a few evenings this summer for me, will you?"

As darkness began to fall on the woods, the seniors gathered around the fire, watching the flames. *It was a good day,* Carol thought as she looked around the group. And as they packed up to leave, Carol felt wonderfully happy, proud of Charlie, proud of Brad, and for some strange reason, proud of herself.

Incident on 49th

No one even knew his name – the boy on the roof. No one knew when he had entered the church or why he had crawled out the window, high above the concrete on 49th Street.

The delivery boy saw him first – saw the blue shirt flapping way up there as the boy crept sideways along the huge expanse of roof.

"Hey! There's a guy up there! Hey, look!" the delivery boy cried, pointing toward the sky.

"Dear God!" said the man selling papers on the corner. "Kid's gonna kill himself! Only reason I know to go up on a roof like that."

A woman in a brown coat paused with a package under her arm, her hands rising slowly to her face. "Oh, no," she breathed, her eyes wide. "Oh, Lord, no!"

A store clerk came out to look. "Not another one!" he said. "Two other guys have jumped off that church in the last five years. I seen 'em both." He shook his head.

"Somebody call the police!" breathed the short man with the black umbrella. "Call the police!"

The boy reached the steeple. Far above the street, as the wind tossed his hair, he began his slow climb to the top, grasping the ornamental projections that stuck out on all sides. Up he went, inch by inch.

Once his foot slipped, and the crowd, now 50 or more, cried out in collective horror. Still the boy moved upward, ignoring the people below.

"He's gonna kill himself, that's for sure," said the delivery boy.

The store clerk nodded. "Yep. Third time in five years. I seen the other two."

There was a wail of a siren and a squad car rounded the corner, slowed down in front of the church, and stopped. Two police officers got out and looked up.

"There he is," said one of them, pointing to the boy on the steeple. He took his whistle from his pocket and blew two shrill blasts.

The boy looked down. The officer brusquely motioned him down. The boy did not move. He looked at the officers and the growing crowd on the sidewalk across the street.

"Come on down!" the officer yelled.

"Come down!" yelled the man from the newstand.

"Come down! Come down!" yelled the crowd, taking up the chant.

The boy on the steeple did not move for a moment. Then he buried his face in his arm and leaned heavily against the tower.

The crowd moaned apprehensively. The second police officer got back in the car and radioed headquarters for help.

Two more squad cars and a rescue truck arrived.

Men climbed out and went inside the church. The minister came out the arched doors and stared up at the roof. Then he, too, went back inside.

"Oh, Jesus, help him!" the woman in the brown coat prayed.

"I saw him first" said the delivery boy. "I was the first to see him! I saw his blue shirt and said to myself, 'That ain't no bird.' "

"He'll jump," said the newspaper man, jingling the change in his pocket. "Only reason I know to be up on a roof like that."

"Three guys in five years," said the store clerk. "I seen 'em all."

There were men on the roof now—men with ropes and a ladder—shirt-sleeved men climbing out a window near the top. Slowly they started across the long roof, single file, on hands and knees.

The boy on the steeple turned around. He saw them coming and let go momentarily, swaying backward. The crowd screamed. The boy caught himself and hung on.

The delivery boy whistled. "Man, he just about had it that time!" He grasped the handlebars of his bike and excitedly bounced the front wheel up and down.

The crowd swelled to a hundred. Cars stopped, and men looked up. Women came out of shops, shielded their eyes, and stood with mouths open. Workers leaned out the windows of upstairs offices. Taxi drivers left their cabs and came over.

The boy on the steeple began to climb again. The men on the roof stopped. A police officer with a bullhorn called out to the boy. Again the men on the roof advanced. Again the boy continued his climb. The men stopped and the boy stopped. The crowd below waited.

Up on the roof another man climbed out the window.

"It's the preacher himself," the delivery boy said.

A policeman took the minister by the arm, and together they crawled across the roof toward the steeple. The boy watched them come. He did not move. At the base of the spire, the minister stood up and held on. He turned his face toward the boy. The minister did not move and the boy did not move. The minister talked and the boy listened.

Down below, the woman in the brown coat looked at her watch. "I've got a dental appointment at two," she said aloud. "I wish he'd come down." She shifted the package to her other arm.

The delivery boy put his hands to his lips. "Hey, kid!" he bellowed. "You comin' or goin'?"

Some of the people laughed and the delivery boy looked pleased. The boy on the steeple looked down. The delivery boy whistled and waved. The men on the roof began to edge forward again. Suddenly the boy began to climb higher. The men stopped. The boy went on until his left hand touched the top of the steeple. He stopped and rested, his shirt flapping wildly, his face in his arm.

"Cold drinks! Popsicles! Ice-cream bars!" A vendor pushed his white wagon through the crowd. "*Ice-cold Coke.*"

The store clerk gave him a dollar. "Got Pepsi? I'll take a Pepsi."

More people came—men hanging out office windows, smoking cigarettes; waitresses with hands on their hips, nudging each other; wide-eyed boys with Popsicles, staring in excited fascination at the boy on the steeple.

The man with the umbrella went in a store and came back with a pair of binoculars.

"What's happening?" said the woman in the brown coat.

The short man adjusted the lens. "Looks like the minister is talking to him. The kid sure looks scared. Yeah, the kid's crying. Now he's shaking his head."

The men on the roof sat down, waiting. The minister stood motionless, his face turned up toward the boy, talking . . . talking. . . .

The short man with the binoculars got tired and handed them to someone else. "Nice place for a conversation," he said disgustedly.

" 'Fraid to jump and 'fraid to come down," said the store clerk. "Just like the other two. Three guys in five years."

The delivery boy put his hands to his lips. "Hey, what's wrong? You chicken?"

The newspaper man laughed and lit a cigar. "That'll get him, all right."

The delivery boy called again: "Chicken! Chicken!"

"Ice-cold Coke," said the vendor.

"Two here," said the newspaper man. He gave one to the delivery boy.

There were 300 now and the crowd was growing.

"How long's he been up there?" said a girl coming out of a dress shop.

The woman in the brown coat turned around. "Over an hour, and I was supposed to be at the dentist's at two o'clock."

The girl shook her head and said, "Well, if they can't get him down, let him jump. If that's what he wants to do, let him jump."

"I'm 15 minutes late now," said the woman in the brown coat.

Up on the roof, the minister began to climb up the nobby steeple toward the boy. The men at the far end of the roof got up and began crawling across the top. The boy began to climb again and went as far as he could go, kicking frantically at the minister beneath him. The minister climbed back down beside the police officer.

"Aw, for cryin' out loud!" The newspaperman puffed away on his cigar. "Jump or come down, kid–take your choice."

"When you gonna *jump?*" somebody yelled from in back.

"When you gonna jump, chicken?" repeated the delivery boy, laughing.

The boy on the steeple turned his face toward the crowd below.

"*Jump!*" the delivery boy screeched up at him. "C'mon, chicken, jump!"

"Make up your mind!" yelled the store clerk.

"Jump! Jump!" yelled the crowd, laughing.

The minister turned around and looked down. He said something to the police officer, and the officer waved one arm at the crowd. No one paid attention.

"Jump!" the crowd yelled.

"Jump! Jump!"

The boy on the steeple twisted his body around.

"Come on, jump!" yelled the delivery boy. "I ain't got all day."

Suddenly the boy leaned over and spat.

"Jump! Jump! Jump! Jump! Jump! Jump Jump! . . ."

The minister stretched out his hand to the boy above him. The boy leaned back. And suddenly he let go.

For a moment he seemed suspended above the towering steeple, arms outstretched. The crowd hushed. Then suddenly his body catapulted backwards and, without a single sound, he plummeted silently toward the street. A woman screamed, and then it was all over. With a dull *whap,* the boy landed on the concrete on 49th Street, twisted and broken, legs grotesquely askew. The blue shirt flapped no more.

The crowd surged forward, silence in their throats. The woman in the brown coat crossed herself. The man with the black umbrella pressed closer for a better look. The store clerk shook his head and said to no one in particular, "Three of 'em in five years—right here on this corner." The delivery boy wheeled his way through the crowd and stood gaping at the body. "I was the first to see him," he said, "and I knew he wasn't a bird."

A police officer came pushing through the crowd.

"Your number's up, you gotta go. That's the way I

see it," said the girl who had come out of the dress shop.

"Nuthin' we could do," rasped the newspaperman. "Kid's gonna jump, you can't stop 'im."

The police officer reached the broken body on 49th Street. He took off his coat and spread it over the boy, and the crowd turned away.

Everything Today

Kathy paused with her brush halfway through a lock of long, black hair. In the mirror she could see her friend sitting rather straight on the edge of the bed, waiting for her to say something. Finally Kathy spoke the words.

"You're *pregnant?*"

Kim nodded, and Kathy turned completely around. The young girl's eyes looked even bluer than they were because of the thinness of her skin around the temples. Her blonde hair had been combed back and tied with a ribbon. The same old Kim, but something about her expression was different—a bit determined, perhaps—a bit excited—a little bit scared.

"When is it due?" Kathy asked numbly.

"December."

"Does Jason know yet?"

Kim nodded again. Suddenly she drew her legs up and hugged her knees, looking straight at Kathy. "Kathy, I wish you'd say whatever you're thinking. I don't care what it is but *say* it."

"Well, I'm . . . surprised. I don't understand you."

"You can understand about *love*, can't you?"

"I think so. But that doesn't explain everything."

Kim sighed. "I know. And I can't say it was in a fit of passion, because we both clearly knew what we were doing – each time."

"I don't know how much you meant to tell me, Kim, but why did you?"

"There's nobody I'd rather tell." Kim stretched out on the bed and lay looking up at the ceiling with one arm over her forehead. "It's simply that we got *utterly, deathly* sick of waiting, that's all." She closed her eyes and then opened them again. "We've been going together for two years, and we've known for at least one that we want to get married. You can't expect two people who are in love to hold off forever."

"Didn't you worry about getting pregnant?"

"No. We were careful at first. Then, nothing happened and we . . . we simply got careless."

Kathy put down her brush and slowly reached for the hand lotion. "Well," she said finally. "What are you going to do? Have you told your folks?"

"Yes. Mother cried and dad was angry. I've *told* them that this really won't change things so much—we'll just be getting married sooner, that's all—but they're still pretty upset."

When the light was out, the girls lay in bed talking quietly. Kim finally drifted off to sleep, but Kathy stared out at the street lights.

It was hard to believe—Kim, whom she'd known ever since they were in fourth grade, through confirmation and now in League together, and youth choir. . . .

"You can understand about love, can't you?" Kim had asked. Yes, Kathy could understand about love. She'd been going with Steve for over a year and they too had talked about getting married. She knew what it was like to enjoy the warmth of each other's arms, the exciting closeness of talking about intimate things. What had kept her and Steve from going all the way?

Both she and Steve had read a book Pastor Hodges had given them, one about marriage and the start of a good sexual relationship – how it needed freedom from worry and hurry, with as many conditions as possible in its favor. Both of them had wanted their relationship–when the time came–to have all the advantages they could give it.

A few days later, at the breakfast table, Kathy told her parents. Her mother put down her piece of toast and said slowly, "I'm so sorry for her, Kathy!"

Mr. Lowry shook his head disbelievingly. "A high-school senior! I never thought that of Ted Blade's daughter!"

"Mrs. Blade's already talked to the minister, mother," Kathy said quietly. "He's going to marry them during spring vacation and she wants Steve and me to stand up for them. What do you think?"

"Kim was always your best friend dear, and we all think a lot of her. Of course you should stand up for her. I just . . . just feel so terribly sorry."

"What is it that causes young people to lose their perspective?" Dad asked. "They want everything *now*. They want to experience everything there is to life right now, all in one great gulp."

For a while Kathy thought that things would go as

always between the two couples. Jason was quieter than usual, but when the four got together on weekends, the talk turned to the same things that had interested them in the past – the senior play, League activities, television, teachers, and school work. . . .

Somehow, though, it seemed a little strange. The wedding was only two weeks away now. They talked some about it, but not much. And still no mention of the baby among the four of them.

It's *unnatural,* Kathy thought one Saturday evening, looking across the restaurant table at Kim. The young blonde girl sat staring distractedly out the window while Steve and Jason talked sports. *It's like some horrible secret we're keeping!*

A classmate from another table sauntered over as he was leaving. "You're going out for football next fall, aren't you, Jason?"

"Sure would like to . . . but I don't know if I'll be going to college full time."

"It'd be a crying shame if you couldn't, Jason–to waste a talent like that!"

After the boy left, the four sat in awkward silence. Finally the waitress brought the check and they were glad to leave.

On Thursday evening after choir practice, two of the boys came over and cornered Jason as they left the church.

"Listen, Bill's going to get his boat on the lake for spring vacation and all the guys are going up for a fishing trip. What do you say?"

"Wish I could," Jason said, moving toward the car. "But I have something else planned."

"But Jason! You didn't make it up there last year and said to be sure and tell you if we went again this spring."

"I know, but I can't this time. Thanks, anyway, for the invite."

Kim was already in the car and Kathy slipped in quietly and closed the door. Jason got in on the other side and started the motor.

"Jason," Kim began quickly. "I'm sorry you can't go. I know you wanted to last. . . ."

"Oh, I'm not heartbroken," Jason said, pulling out into the street. "That's not the biggest problem."

No one spoke for a moment but Kathy could feel the tenseness. Finally Kim said, "What *is* the biggest problem, Jason?"

"I didn't mean to say it that way."

"Well, tell me, I want to know."

"Forget it, Kim."

"I can't! You're thinking about college, aren't you? But you'll get through. I mean, just because you'll be married. . . ."

"Sure I'll get through . . . in eight or ten years . . . part-time."

"*Couldn't* you go full time? Isn't there some way we could manage?"

Jason gave a quick laugh. "A full-time job, full-time school, a wife, *and* a baby? That's all I need! And what about you? You wanted college, too!"

Kathy froze. Kim didn't even seem to be breathing. Jason shifted uncomfortably, unable to break the silence.

"I've got to buy a few things at the drugstore," Kathy blurted out. "Why don't you let me off here?"

Chuck slowed the car to a stop.

"Thanks for the lift," Kathy said, and she hurried into the store.

She headed for the lunch counter and took a booth near the back. With her face buried in her hands, she prayed, "God, help them through it. *Please* help them through it!"

"Order, miss?" asked the skinny woman standing over her.

"Could I just have a glass of water, please?"

The water came and the waitress shuffled away again.

Kathy closed her eyes. It was only two months ago that they'd talked about college and all the things they wanted to do together—the four of them. Then came the night Kim told her about the baby, and the morning Kim vomited at school and Kathy had made up the excuse about stomach flu. Now, less than two weeks before the wedding, this quarrel.

It was almost 10 o'clock when she looked at her watch. She got up quickly, ignored the quizzical look of the waitress, and walked home. When she started up the sidewalk, she saw a forlorn figure huddled on the steps.

"Kim!" she said as she walked up and sat down beside her friend.

Kim buried her face in her lap. "Oh, K . . . Kathy!" she sobbed bitterly.

Kathy wanted desperately to comfort her, but there was nothing to say—just nothing to say.

"He . . . he . . . he's *sorry,* Kathy! He didn't say so, b . . . but I can tell! He wishes that . . . he wishes that. . . ."

"That you weren't pregnant?" Kathy finished gently.

Kim nodded violently and again drowned a sob in her lap.

"Well," Kathy said finally. "It means a pretty big change in his life – yours too – and maybe he'll just have to get used to the idea gradually. But you know he loves you."

"But I wanted him to *want* our baby. I . . . I wanted him to be glad about it and glad we were getting married. I looked forward to this for so long. . . ."

The front door opened and Mrs. Lowry came out and looked around in the darkness. "Oh, Kathy! I *thought* I heard voices out here! Won't you girls catch cold?"

"I'll be in in a minute, Mother."

"Jason's on the phone and wants to know if Kim is here. He said he'd be right over if she was, so I'll tell him." She went back inside.

In what seemed only a minute or two, Jason's car pulled up in front. He hurried up the sidewalk.

"Kim," he said gently, sitting down by her. "I . . . I've been pretty upset. I'm sorry–really sorry! Come on and let me take you home."

"Go on, Kim. I'll see you tomorrow," Kathy said.

Kim stood up and leaned heavily against Jason. He put his arm around her and they started down the steps.

Kathy stood in the darkness of the doorway and watched them go. They did love each other. All they had meant to do was to give comfort and happiness to each other. They had wanted to share all that was possible. They had wanted everything today.

Those Who Think Young

Back in 1930, Grandpa Grinager was known as the cat's pajamas. Today he might still have been in style except that he was 69, not 16, and had arthritis of the knees or something.

He was far from senile. Every morning he did his exercises—no deep knee bends, to be sure, but he performed a few calisthenics and managed a push-up or two if the weather was dry. Then he went downstairs and fried an egg, the only thing he'd learned to cook since Grandma Grinager died, and usually finished breakfast off with store-bought pie.

After that his day consisted of going down to the drugstore, chatting with friends, listening to a ball game or doing a bit of gardening. Then he'd change his clothes and go down to the Chinese-American restaurant for supper or over to Fifth Street for spaghetti. And finally, he'd round up the evening with a good detective story.

This, however, was all BJR—*before Jim and Rita,* ages 18 and 16 respectively. Meg, Gramps' daughter, had persuaded him to move in with her and Ralph and the children, and it had seemed like a good idea.

And so he came from Connecticut to Baltimore and was installed in a little room all his own near the front of the house, "where he could watch the cars go by," as Meg put it. And that's about all he did. The family accepted him as one accepts an antique and treated him accordingly.

"Good grief, Gramps!" said Rita when she found him walking around the house in his bare feet. "You want to get pneumonia or something?" And after hearing this five or six times, Grandpa Grinager decided maybe there was a pain somewhere in his chest so he put on the wool slippers Rita had made him for Christmas.

"C'mon, Gramps, let's go for a drive," Jim would say, taking his grandfather's elbow as he ushered him down to the car. Then they'd drive out in the country to see all the peaceful brown cows eating peaceful green grass and Grandpa Grinager would wonder what people in Baltimore did for excitement anyway. He'd end up falling asleep, and Jim would figure it had been too much for him. So the next time they'd skip the cows and concentrate on cornfields, which Gramps hoped never to see again as long as he lived.

Sometimes the family would take Gramps to dinner. They passed up the pizza parlors and the Oriental food places and the Eastern cuisine restaurants and took him to a dreary little place called Mrs. Ritter's Kitchen, where the most exciting thing on the menu was meat loaf. They worried about his digestion and even had *him* wondering if lemon meringue and sauerkraut were too much for a man his age.

At church on Sunday morning, Gramps would stand outside with Rita before the service, and all her friends would ask if he thought it would rain. Grandpa Grinager didn't know, didn't care, and began to wonder if the younger generation mistook him for a barometer.

And just when he'd been waiting all week to watch the Miss America pageant on television, he discovered that the young people were monopolizing the TV that night and had thoughtfully bought him a book of crossword puzzles.

"But, Kathy, he's practically 70!" Rita said to her girl friend. "He needs his rest! Turn the TV down!"

And so Gramps, enjoying the sounds of the TV that came drifting into his bedroom, heard the music cut short, and promptly fell asleep out of sheer boredom.

Something, he decided, *had to be done.* He could practically feel himself shriveling up, from his ankles to his elbows, and bones that had never hurt before were hurting now. He was even getting pains in his false teeth.

Obviously, he had to change his image. He could always buy a green felt hat and yellow vest. He could take karate lessons or join a scuba class at the Y. But as it turned out, nothing quite so drastic was necessary.

It was a fine Saturday morning. When Gramps got out of bed, he decided it would be a lot more fun to do push-ups in his underwear than in his clothes; so he pulled down the blinds and did his calisthenics. Afterward, he sat down in the rocking chair to decide whether to walk over to the park or the courthouse, and covered himself with a quilt while he thought about it. He'd just decided to go to the Pancake House instead for a stack of strawberry pancakes when Rita tapped on the door and stuck her head inside.

"Your oatmeal's ready, Gramps," she called.

"Don't think I want any this morning, Rita," he said, wondering if he should tell her about the strawberry pancakes. But Rita was gone; so he closed his eyes again and wondered if maybe blueberry wouldn't taste better. Or pecan or peanut butter.

Rita, meanwhile, dashed into the kitchen, her eyes wide. "Mother," she cried, "he's sitting there in his chair with a blanket around him and the shades drawn and he doesn't want to eat!"

The next thing Gramps knew, the family was gathered outside his door and he heard Ralph say, "What's the matter with him? You sure he's breathing?"

"He won't eat or anything!" Rita exclaimed. "He won't even look out the window."

They all peeped in. Gramps didn't move. He even tried holding his breath and counting to 15. And when he got to 12, he had a most wonderful idea. He almost chuckled out loud.

"Gramps," said Meg, "wouldn't you like to go out for a little air this morning?"

Gramps tried not to laugh as he made his voice waver. "No, Meg, I think I'll just sit here in my chair today."

"No oatmeal, Gramps? Can I bring you a tray?"

"No, I'm not hungry . . . nothing at all," Grandpa Grinager replied, wondering if they could hear his stomach rumbling beneath the blanket. Pineapple. Pineapple pancakes. That would have been perfect.

What happened next was exactly what he predicted. The doctor arrived. Gramps fully intended to let him in on his little joke, but Meg hovered around the door, so he couldn't.

"He's fit as a fiddle, physically," he heard the doctor tell her in the hall. "Sometimes it's just plain senility and they're better off in a nursing home. But if I were you, I'd try to snap him out of it. The trouble with Gramps is he thinks he's too old to have any fun in life. (Gramps almost choked laughing.) You've got to convince him he's well and strong. Get him interested in bright, lively things. Persuade him to go to new places, see new things. It's worth a try."

Good ole Doc, Gramps thought, settling back in his chair and wiggling his toes in anticipation. *This is going to be fun.*

At eleven o'clock Jim bounded in. "C'mon, Gramps, let's go for a drive."

"You go on alone, Jim," said Gramps. "I'm feeling sort of weak."

"Oh, no," said Jim. "C'mon. It'll do you good." He pulled off the blanket and pulled Gramps from the chair.

"How about a ride out in the country?" said Jim, once they were in the car.

Cows, thought Gramps. Stupid, peaceful cows—chewing, chewing, chewing. . . .

"That will be fine, Jim," he said, leaning back and closing his eyes. "So quiet, so peaceful. . . ."

Jim swung the car around. "Changed my mind, Gramps," he said: "Gonna take you down to the docks and watch the boats unload."

Now you're talking, Gramps thought, his eyes open again, and he felt like taking the wheel himself to get there faster.

Afterward, they were both starved. As Jim headed over toward Mrs. Ritter's Kitchen he suddenly veered off to the left.

"Gramps, you ever eat pizza?" he asked.

Should I tell him? Gramps wondered. *Should I confess to putting away several dozen mushroom and anchovy creations in the last two years?*

"Pizza?" said Grandpa Grinager. "Must be Italian, huh?"

This time Gramps could not contain himself. Jim stared as he devoured six pieces. He could scarcely wait to get home and tell the others.

"Mom, he's like a new man!" Gramps heard Jim say in the kitchen. "He forgot all about his arthritis and his stomach! He didn't even seem old anymore!"

Rita took over next. She rearranged Gramp's room, persuaded him to get a different haircut, and bought him a pocket-size stereo set with headphones. Then Meg got him to join a bowling league, and Ralph bought him a jogging suit.

Grandpa Grinager let them have their way. He accompanied Jim to Saturday afternoon football practice, and jogged with Rita in the park. He was constantly exhorted to wear bright colors, read good books, and visit new places. He was having the time of his life!

"You've no idea what we've done for him!" he overheard Rita telling her girl friend over the phone. "Why, he was moping around as though he were 97 or something, and you should see him now!"

"Just had to be convinced he wasn't old," Jim was heard to say from the front porch. "A man will just shrivel up if you let him sit around thinking about his aches all day. Teach him to think young! That's all he needed!"

And Grandpa Grinager, sitting inside with a detective book and a bag of pretzels, smiled, zipped up his sweatshirt, and decided to jog down the street for a frozen yogurt.

Scenes for a Small Cast

PROLOG

Mr. Preston: Sex? A necessary part of life—for a man at least, and beginning at an early age. That's why I worry about Connie and the boys she dates. Who knows what really goes on? A father can't follow his daughter around.

Mrs. Preston: Sex? It's the most sacred part of marriage. But outside of marriage it's cheap, degrading, and ugly. Ron's a nice boy, but he's been seeing Connie a lot, and . . . well, they're bound to feel intimate when they're together so much. When she first started dating, she'd tell me all about it later. She doesn't do that anymore.

Grandma Talbot: Sex? Well, in my day we didn't talk about it outside of marriage, and we didn't say too much inside marriage either. Like it or not, it's God's plan for populating the earth and I suppose a girl ought to know what she's in for before she's married. But the way Connie and Ron carry on! I don't know why Helen allows it. The way they sit all tangled up on the sofa! I can imagine what they do in private.

Connie Preston: Sex? I've never experienced it, really. All I know is what I feel when I think about Ron—the sensations, the feelings—they're wonderful! I don't know why mom never talks about them. It's like a physiology lesson with her. Sometimes I wonder what it really will be like for me. Do all girls have these feelings? Sometimes I think mom would be embarrassed if she knew.

Ron Holmes: Sex? Well, I can't tell you from personal experience, but I'll bet it's great. Sometimes when I think about Connie I go nuts, and I think she feels the same way. All the time we spend alone together doesn't help any. We sit down in the family room after her folks have gone to bed and spend the rest of the evening pretending to watch TV and telling ourselves to stop.

SCENE ONE

A Saturday morning. The Preston family is having breakfast. Connie comes to the table late, preoccupied with a quarrel she had with Ron the night before and worried about their date for the evening.

Grandma Talbot: Well! Can't you even manage a smile, Connie? Or did you get home so late you're still half asleep?

Connie: Not any later than usual. *(She begins eating silently.)*

Mrs. Preston: I thought I heard you drive in around 11:00, dear. It sounded as though you were standing outside a long time talking. Didn't you ask Ron in?

CONNIE: I suppose you heard everything we said.

MRS. PRESTON: I wouldn't listen in, dear. I thought you knew that. Of course, if you want to tell us anything, I hope you will.

CONNIE *(impatiently)*: Tell you what, for heaven's sake? Good grief, can't I have any privacy? Did you have to give a running account of everything you did when you were my age?

GRANDMA TALBOT: Helen didn't carry on the way you do, young lady. Why, if I'd ever seen her kissing a boy in public, I'd have. . . .

MR. PRESTON: Be quiet, mother, will you? I'd like to finish my coffee in peace. *(Turns to Connie.)* Of course you're entitled to privacy, honey. It's just that we can't help worrying sometimes, that's all. Boys being what they are. . . .

CONNIE: Which is what?

MR. PRESTON: Well . . . you know. Impetuous. Hard to hold off. And I don't suppose Ron is any exception.

CONNIE: You always make Ron sound like a beast. Don't you think he has any feelings for me besides sexual ones? Don't you think he wants what's best for both of us? I've got sexual feelings too, you know.

MR. PRESTON: That's supposed to make me feel better?

GRANDMA TALBOT: Honestly, Helen, it embarrasses me to sit here and listen to her.

CONNIE: Then why don't you go to your room, grandma?

MRS. PRESTON: Connie!

CONNIE (*jumping up*): Well, I will then! You want me to talk, and when I do you leap all over me! It doesn't make any difference – you believe what you want to anyway.

SCENE TWO

Saturday night. Ron and Connie have eaten in a small restaurant and are sitting side by side in a corner booth.

RON: Connie, I'm sorry about last night. It was part my fault.

CONNIE (*half smiling*): Which part?

RON: Well, not the shorts you were wearing, that's for sure. And not the way you lay in my lap.

CONNIE: So I suppose it's my fault you were so free with your hands?

RON: I didn't say that. But you helped.

CONNIE (*more gently*): I know. It's stupid to lead you on and then get all upset. It's like I'm ashamed to admit that I like it too. I put all the blame on you.

RON: That's a big help. (*They laugh a little and are silent.*)

CONNIE: You know, we don't even know where we'll be three years from now. We might be in different colleges halfway across the country. Marriage seems like a hundred years away. Sometimes I . . . I feel so close to you, I don't care what happens.

RON: Sure you do. And I care what happens too. I don't want it to be one night or two hours in a motel room. I want us to be able to be with each other the next morning and the next afternoon too, if we feel like it. I want us to have a private place where we don't have to hide or lie about who we are.

CONNIE: So do I. That's the way I've always thought about it. But it doesn't help much now, does it?

RON: No.

CONNIE: You know, I just can't have a normal conversation about sex with mom and dad. Mom always says sex is beautiful, but she never says it's fun.

RON: Well, they're entitled to some privacy, too.

CONNIE: I know. Sometimes I really envy them—the way they can be together any time they like. I guess there's no good solution to being young and unmarried—having to stop every time you feel yourself getting close to someone.

SCENE THREE

Late Saturday night. Connie and Ron arrive home a half hour past curfew to find the Prestons waiting up.

MR. PRESTON: Connie, do you realize it's after midnight?

CONNIE: I'm sorry. We were talking, and just didn't notice it was so late until we left the park.

MRS. PRESTON *(stiffly)*: The park?

CONNIE: Yes. We were just driving around talking.

MRS. PRESTON: I see.

RON: It's my fault about the time. I was the only one with a watch, and I should have paid attention.

MR. PRESTON: She's always had a good reputation, Ron. I'd hate to see her lose it.

CONNIE: Dad!

RON: So would I, Mr. Preston. Listen, Connie, I'll call you tomorrow. *(Ron leaves, and Mr. Preston starts up the stairs.)*

MR. PRESTON: Well, we've wasted enough sleep. Let's all get to bed.

MRS. PRESTON *(following Connie upstairs)*: And I thought I could trust you! Look at your hair! That's all you and Ron think about—sneaking off somewhere by yourselves. I'd be ashamed!

CONNIE *(turning around and facing her mother on the landing)*: Ashamed of what?

MR. PRESTON: Oh, for heaven's sake, Connie, go to bed and think about it. Do you have to have things spelled out?

Connie goes to her room and lies down on her bed, hurt, angry, and embarrassed. She cries silently for awhile, her hands over her face. The door opens and Mrs. Preston steps halfway in.

MRS. PRESTON: Connie, I'm sorry I was so accusing. It's just that I worry so about you. Sometimes you seem so involved with Ron and your feelings about each other—I just don't want you to make a mistake, that's all.

Connie silently rolls over and reaches for a tissue.

MRS. PRESTON: Is there anything at all you'd like to talk about? I'll try to understand. I really will.

CONNIE: No. I'd just like to go to sleep. Nothing

happened between Ron and me tonight that you'd be ashamed of, and if you don't believe me—well, I can't help that.

MRS. PRESTON: All right. I believe you. But . . . sometime, can't we talk?

EPILOG

Five people lie awake, thinking private thoughts.

CONNIE: Well, it wasn't a lie. We didn't do anything tonight she'd be ashamed of. How can you go out with boys always feeling ashamed if you're close, and then someday marry somebody and not feel ashamed anymore? Mom says that's all we think about. Well, why not? I don't know—she looked so sad standing here. Maybe I should have talked with her. She was young once too. She must have felt something. I suppose she imagines all kinds of horrible things happening to me. Maybe tomorrow, when grandma's not around, I could talk with her a little—just to see.

MRS. PRESTON: If only I could reach her. I love her so much, and yet there's this wall between us. Sometimes I think I worry too much about her, and other times I'm afraid I don't worry enough. Sometimes I think she looks at me like I'm a perfect loon for trusting her so much, and other times I think she hates me for questioning her. If only we could talk. . . .

MR. PRESTON: "Ashamed of what?" Connie asked. Well, if she's not, she should be. And she tells me she's got sexual feelings, too. What am I supposed to say to that? Still . . . she's only being honest. I don't really want her to be cold and indifferent to sex when she grows up, do I? How will she keep the lid on it till she's married? How did we?

RON: I don't know who's more mixed up—me or society. Take a cold shower, that's what a guy's supposed to do. Well, there's never a cold shower handy when you need it—just a warm, flesh-and-blood girl and a thousand rules about where you can put your hands and where you can't. Would I have gone all the way the other night if Connie had let me? I don't know. . . . It's not fair to make her be the one to say no.

GRANDMA TALBOT: It's a different world these kids are growing up in. Sometimes I look at Connie and her young man and the way they talk so easy with each other, and I think maybe I missed something. Maybe I didn't feel that easy with Albert in my whole life, and that's a pity, I suppose. Helen says if only she could talk with the girl. . . . Well, she's her daughter, not mine. I wouldn't know . . . I wouldn't know at all what to say.

CURTAIN

Time Out

It was the sun hitting his eyes that woke him. Then he felt the cold concrete under his shoulders. A newspaper had blown across the school yard during the night and settled up against him. He felt like a bum.

Greg sat up, moved his stiff legs, and ran his hands through his hair. His mouth felt like an old shoe. He picked up his gym bag and his father's army duffle bag and walked around to the water fountain by the swings. He couldn't stay here another night. He might get mugged. And September was just around the corner.

He had stuffed everything he possibly could into the two bags and left the house at three in the morning last Wednesday. It was Saturday now. The police would be looking for him if his parents had reported him missing. Did they care enough, he wondered, to make the report? Yes, that much at least. . . .

Greg walked back to the steps and unwrapped some cheese crackers he had bought the day before. What could he do now? School was a week off. He had to have some place to stay. The only thing he was sure of was that he wouldn't go home.

He leaned back and closed his eyes against the sun. If his parents beat him, the authorities would step in and find him a foster home. But when the abuse was emotional, when only his spirit had been broken, it seemed there was nothing anyone could do.

For 15 years he'd taken it. For 15 years his mother came and went, and even during the times she stayed, she was threatening to leave, so it was never a surprise when he came home and found her gone.

"I can't take it anymore," she would scream.

What about me? Greg had always wondered at ages eight, eleven, twelve, and fourteen. *How long do you think I can stand it? What are your plans for me?*

But he never asked her that because he was afraid of the answer. He had never been wanted in the first place. He heard it over and over again in endless variations.

What it was that his mother couldn't stand, he was never sure—him, her husband, her marriage, even herself perhaps. Everything seemed to upset her. When she left, Greg's father became depressed, moody, irritable, and remained silent for days. But at least there was peace—of a sort.

When they were home together, they verbally attacked each other and then, when they tired of that, they attacked Greg. He was stupid, inept, lazy, they said. And Greg began to wonder if it was true. He had heard it all his life. He was no brain, no genius, but he did a passable job at school and had never been in serious trouble. They expected more out of him than that, however, or perhaps out of life, or marriage, or even themselves.

You can't let your parents' immaturities ruin your own life, Greg, the school counselor had repeated again and again during their weekly sessions last spring. *Never believe that what they say about you is true. If they didn't have you to kick around, they'd find another target. Do you have any relatives you could live with for the next few years?*

No, there were no relatives except an invalid grandmother in Ohio and some uncles and cousins in New York he rarely saw. Not much of a clan. Not much of a family. And so when the fight was on last Tuesday night and the air was filled with accusations, Greg had gone in his room and locked the door. And at three the next morning, when the house was quiet at last, he left.

A squad car moved slowly along the road. Greg knew he couldn't stay on the school steps forever. He hid his bags behind a wall and headed for a fast food place for something to eat. His head felt groggy and his thoughts spun wildly, as though they had been going around and around in his head all night.

It would be so simple if his parents hated him 100%. It would be so easy if they were beyond rehabilitation, if they simply didn't care.

But they did. When his mother came home from an extended stay, she was remorseful, temporarily loving, laden with guilt, and seemed, for a few days or weeks at least, to be able to see into Greg's soul and know what she was doing to him.

"I'm sorry, Greg," she would weep. "I've got so many problems of my own I can't handle yours, too."

"Greg," his dad would say, "if it looks like I don't care, I do. It happened to me when I was growing up, and I suppose it'll go on happening until somebody breaks the chain."

"Then let's all go for counseling together," Greg would say. "Let's call for an appointment right now. Pastor Marks said we could come anytime."

But his parents could never bring themselves to do it. At the very suggestion each accused the other of needing it most, and the idea was so threatening that it ended in another battle, and Greg would wonder why he bothered.

He picked up his order and sat down in a booth. *What were they doing now?* he wondered. He had never left home before, though he could not understand why not. They would be frantic. They might even call the pastor they had avoided for so long. Their guilt would overwhelm them.

Let it, he muttered quickly, stuffing the toast in his mouth. *Let them suffer even a fraction of what I've put up with all these years.*

He went to the counter and got change for a dollar, and then went to the pay phone to call a friend. He needed to talk with someone. He felt the need to touch bases, to let someone know where he was.

"Greg!" said a sleepy voice at the other end. "What time is it? Where are you?"

"I guess it is pretty early. A little after eight. I'm down at McDonald's."

"Man, the police were here last night asking questions about you. Your parents are really upset. . . ."

"I don't care, Tom. You know the story. . . ."

"Yeah, I do. . . ."

"I'm not sure why I'm calling. I guess I'd like to ask if I could sort of camp out in your garage for awhile. I've got to have some place to stay. I was thinking I could get a job after school and pay for my food. . . ."

"Listen, Greg, you can stay here in the house. Mom was talking about it last night after the police left. I told her what you've been going through. . . ."

"Are you sure, Tom? I'd help pay my way. . . ."

"Sure I'm sure. I'll tell her you're coming."

There were good people in the world, Greg thought as he hung up. Whatever happened, let him never forget that. No matter what his parents did about their own problems, let him never go through life reacting to every teacher or boss as though they were his dad, or every female as his mother. And if he ever married, let him be the one to break the chain.

Dear God, he prayed, *help me break the chain.*

And then, as he stared at the coins in his hand, he turned back to the phone again and called home.

"Greg!" his mother wept, "we want you to come home."

"I'll be all right, mom," he said. "But I'm not coming back for awhile, not until we get some help, but I just wanted you to know that I'll keep in touch. . . ."

The Rivals

"Not again!"

The woman in the faded slippers turned toward Shelley and put one hand on her hip where her blouse bulged out over her skirt top.

Shelley stopped and looked at her mother. Strange how she'd never noticed how full her mother looked around the chin and neck.

"Again?" she replied. "Just choir practice, that's all."

Mrs. Lawson turned away, poking at a wisp of hair that hung down her neck. "Seems to me you're out all the time—dates, parties, play rehearsal. . . ."

"Haven't got a thing going for Saturday," Shelley said, pulling on her jacket. "I'll be home all day, and you'll be sick of looking at me." She hurried outside and on up the street toward the church.

The May breeze caught her hair and swirled it around her cheeks, but Shelley walked with her head down, staring at the sidewalk. She felt angry inside, a feeling that was becoming more persistent. She felt betrayed by the person who had always been closest to her.

Until a year or so ago, she and her mother had enjoyed a great relationship. Shelley had always felt lucky that they could talk like they did. Mrs. Lawson was as interested in whether her daughter would make the play or the school newspaper as Shelley was herself.

Not anymore. Now, when she came home from school to recount the day's events, Shelley felt a certain reserve on her mother's part, a subtle annoyance, as though she resented Shelley's activities.

What had come over mom, anyway? She even looked different. She'd gained a little weight—maybe that was it. Well, that was her problem. Shelley had enough worries about her own figure and complexion.

Because she still had her head down, she bumped into Greg, who was waiting for her in front of the church.

"Hey, you're supposed to be looking up at the stars on a night like this, not down at your feet," he kidded.

"Sorry," she laughed. "My feet are so big I have to make sure I don't fall over them, that's all."

Mr. Coretti was passing out the anthem as Shelley took her seat.

"Glad you're here, Shelley," he said. "Sunday is Mother's Day and we're doing a special number. Will you sing the alto solo for us?"

"I'll try," Shelley said, and instantly wondered what mom would think about it. At one time Mrs. Lawson would have been proud of her. But now

Shelley could almost see her sitting there in the side pew, the corners of her mouth stiff. It was as though her mother didn't like her anymore, and that was a strange and terrible feeling.

On Saturday, Shelley put on a pair of old jeans and a wrinkled shirt, remembering her promise to wash the downstairs windows. She gave her long hair a few licks with the brush and went down to have a piece of toast.

"You look like a mess," Mrs. Lawson said from the corner of the breakfast nook where she was wrapped in a yellow robe.

Shelley stopped in her tracks, not daring to look at her mother. Not "Good morning" or "Nice day, isn't it?" but, "You look like a mess." Mom actually seemed to relish finding fault with her.

She pressed her lips together in an effort to keep her voice in control, then answered tersely, "I promised I'd wash the windows."

Mrs. Lawson retreated. "Oh, I forgot."

Neither one said anything more. The silence in the kitchen was broken only by the rustle of her mother's paper. Shelley sat across the table, sipping her juice, feeling furious. *Mom couldn't be mentally ill, could she?* she thought. *Was this the way it started—the first signs?*

Mr. Lawson came into the kitchen and Shelley welcomed his warm smile—it was such a change from her mother.

"Hi, sweetheart," he said to Shelley. "Beautiful day, isn't it? Perfect spring weather." He poured a cup of coffee, then stood at the window looking out over the yard. "Almost wish I had a vegetable garden. On a day like this I could enjoy hoeing and planting." He turned around again and noticed the sunlight on Shelley's hair.

"Shelley, your hair just sparkles in that sunshine," he said. "That's your best feature. Where did we get a daughter with blond hair, Louise? Nobody on my side of the family has it."

Mrs. Lawson's face showed no expression. "You should have seen mine when I was 16—a lot lighter than Shelley's. And longer, too."

"So I married a blonde and didn't know it," Mr. Lawson smiled. "Give me the sports section, Louise, and I'll read it out on the patio."

Shelley sat at the table, her eyes on her mother. Good grief! The woman was jealous! *Jealous!* She sounded like a disgruntled girl friend, not a mature, 43-year-old mother!

She started to take a bite of toast, then lowered it again, amazed at her discovery. Mom—who had been her idol since she was old enough to walk—was envious of *her!* For 16 years Shelley had tried to look like mom, laugh like mom, cook like mom—and now her mother couldn't stand her because she was succeeding.

The betrayal seemed complete. All these years Shelley had supposed that the older she got, the more she and her mother would have in common. Instead, the gulf between them stretched wider than ever. Shelley picked up her dishes and dumped them in the sink, the cup clattering to the floor.

"For heaven's sake, Shelley, do you have to be so

clumsy?" Mrs. Lawson snapped. "You walk in here looking like a garbage collector and now you bang the dishes around like trash cans."

Shelley turned and faced her mother. "Sorry if my existence annoys you," she said coldly, and went upstairs to put on her shoes.

It wasn't fair. Mom had had her chance at growing up—at being a teenager—at being a woman. She had had her time for dating and parties and popularity. Why should she begrudge Shelley hers?

Mom wasn't mentally ill, she was selfish. She had loved Shelley as long as she had been a gawky, ponytailed girl with freckles on her shoulders. But now that Shelley was getting rounder and feminine and attractive, mom's feelings had changed.

Shelley swept downstairs, grabbed the rags and window cleaner from the closet and went outside. Okay, if that's the way she wanted it. What girl wanted to spend her whole life with her mother anyway? Ahead of her lay college and falling in love and getting married. She could go the rest of her life on her own, if necessary. At least she still had dad.

The fact that tomorrow was Mother's Day only added to the irony. Shelley clung to the top of the stepladder and made large half-circles on the pane with her cloth. Luckily she had bought mom's present last week, for she was in no mood to buy her one today. She'd wrap it up and force herself to smile at mom as she handed it to her, because that was the tradition. But she wasn't fooling herself. She knew how things stood between them.

She stopped working about 11:00 and went in to rest

and wrap the present. Leaving her shoes at the back door, she padded through the kitchen and into the front hallway. She was just about to go upstairs when she caught sight of her mother in the living room and stopped.

Mrs. Lawson was sitting by the front window, still in her robe, and the double chin that Shelley had noticed only two days ago hung over the collar. On her lap sat half a grapefruit in a bowl, her perpetual diet. There was something about the expression on her mother's face, the slump of her shoulders, perhaps, that caught Shelley's attention before she turned and went softly upstairs. What was it she had felt just then? Pity?

She took the package from her closet shelf—a pair of leather gloves—and sat down at her desk to wrap it. Somewhere in her drawer was a Mother's Day card she had purchased weeks ago. She opened the drawer and rummaged through it.

Suddenly she stopped and stared down at an old photograph she had kept in her desk. It showed Shelley with her mother four years before. Shelley, in knee socks, with braces on her teeth, was smiling a much-too-wide grin. But her mother was beautiful, the way Shelley always used to think of her. She wore a soft blue jersey dress, and her long hair, wrapped loosely about her head, shone in the sunlight. Her smile was warm and natural, and she had one arm around Shelley.

For the first time, Shelley realized that her mother was growing older—not just growing, but looking it, too. Mom had gained at least 15 pounds since then, despite her periodic diets. Her face was fuller, the lines about the eyes were deeper, and the sparkle in her hair had been replaced with gray. It had happened so gradually that Shelley had not noticed it.

But her mother, who looked in the mirror every day, saw the lines deepen. For her, aging was real and immediate, and the presence of a young, talented, and pretty daughter only made her more aware of all that she was losing.

It was easy to say that she had had her chance at youth, and that now it was Shelley's turn. But when Shelley was 43, would she feel any different? Would she have no pangs realizing that much of her life was over? Would she feel no envy of a young girl—even her own—who had all of her life yet before her?

Shelley found the Mother's Day card and signed her name to it. She thought of all the times mom had stood by her in the past—the time she had had a fear of going to bed, the summer she broke her collarbone, the year a clique at school turned against her. Patiently mom had let her know that she had the love of her parents and that they would stand by her while she worked her problems through. Couldn't she do the same for mom? Now that her mother needed the assurance of her family that she was still loved, couldn't Shelley wait out the difficult time?

In a rush of tenderness toward her mother, she opened the card and wrote "love" above her name. Mom hadn't been her idol for nothing. The next few months would be difficult, and there would be many times that mom would seem to reject her. But somehow Shelley was going to let her mother know that 43 wasn't the end of the world and would patiently wait for better times when she and mom would be friends again.

A Brief Visit Back

That's all it was going to be. Just long enough to taste mom's apple cake and talk to dad and take Kenny fishing on the coast. Then he would tell them he was going back to Washington.

The bus droned steadily on down the highway. Everything was green or gray—mostly gray: the rocky hills on the side of the road, the pavement, the sky, the houses that hadn't been painted for 35 years. For long stretches there was nothing but dead trees, standing like ghosts against a colorless sky.

Eric closed his eyes. How did people stand it? Of all the places in the United States, why did they pick a small Maine town as close as they could get to nowhere and as far as they could get from lights and life and people?

"Where'd you say you've been this year?" the driver asked over his shoulder.

"Washington, D.C. I stayed with my uncle and finished my senior year of high school there."

The driver nodded. "Must seem different bein' back."

Eric wanted to tell him he'd been waiting all his life to get out and see what the rest of the country was like. But the driver went on. "I been on this route for 22 years, and I wouldn't have any other. This is God's chosen country up here."

Eric leaned back and swallowed. If this was God's chosen country, he'd like to see some place God had rejected.

The bus rolled around the bend and began slowing down – past the potato fields, past old Mr. Perry's barn, now dilapidated – and came to a stop just beyond the clump of birch trees where a small group of smiling people waited.

"Your folks are sure glad to see you, boy," the driver said, as Eric picked up his bags.

"Yeah," said Eric, practicing his lie. "It's sure good to be home."

They swarmed around him like bees and kept stopping all the way home to show him off.

There was apple cake for supper, as he'd expected, and chicken and chowder and new potatoes with peas. This he had honesty missed, and when he told his mother so, she squeezed his hand and said, "Oh, Eric, it's *so* good having you home again. Won't the summer go fast, Kenny, with Eric around?'"

No, he couldn't tell them yet. Wait a couple days till the excitement wore off. Then he'd casually say he knew where he could get a job in Washington for the summer, and that Uncle Clyde had said he was welcome to stay on. After that, of course, Eric would be going to the university, and from then on he'd be on his own. The family couldn't expect a college man to spend a whole summer at home.

They sat on the porch that night eating strawberries and watching the cars go by. Eric told them about Washington – about his visit to the Supreme Court and the Jefferson Memorial. He told them about the cherry blossoms in April and the speedboat regatta in September and the restaurant with a thatched roof that served punch with gardenias in it.

Mrs. Weller shook her head in amazement, and Eric's father sat grinning from the rocking chair. But it was Kenny who was hungriest to hear what Eric said.

"You really saw the president?" he gulped in admiration.

"Well, I was standing outside the gate at the White House, and he was walking around inside. We all put out our hands, but he didn't get to me."

"But–he *might* have shaken your hand," said Kenny.

That night, as he lay in the room he shared with Kenny, Eric felt all the old emptiness return. How often he had lain here before, staring up at the shadowy pattern of light on the ceiling, and wishing with all his heart he were anywhere but here. He remembered how he had tagged along after anyone who had been any place at all. He'd even envied the truck drivers who roared through the lonely little town, his eyes fastened on the license plates to see where they were from.

The next day, while Eric checked the tackle box,

Kenny stood gaping after a car that had just driven by on the highway.

"Hey, Eric, that was a Mazda RX7! What a car!" Kenny exclaimed.

Mrs. Weller handed them a basket that smelled of home-baked bread. "You should hear them around here, Eric – you'd think this was New York or something – roaring and racing down the roads."

"Civilization's moving in, eh?" Eric said. He picked up the lunch basket and gave Kenny the bait. "Well, we're off, mom. Have the skillet ready when we come back."

"They're bitin' good north a bit," called Eric's father.

The pier was warm and wood-smelly. Underneath, the gray-green water lapped and splashed and showered the brothers with its salty spray when the wind was right. They each sat against a post, baited their hooks, and tossed their lines out beyond the breakers. Then they settled down in the sun to wait.

Eric asked about the friends he knew. Where was John Butler? Tim Pollard? Tina Moreno? John was working in Machias, Kenny told him. Tim had hitchhiked to California for the summer. Tina was at her sister's in Philadelphia.

It figures, Eric thought. *Everyone wants to get away.*

"You remember Ron Butler–John's brother?" Kenny asked. Eric nodded. "We get along good."

"What do you do?"

"Oh, just hang around – you know. Sometimes he gets his cousin's car."

"You don't have a license," Eric reminded.

Kenny laughed. "Oh, we don't take it on the main roads – just back-country. Man, you should see it, Eric. It really moves!"

Eric listened silently. This wasn't the Kenny he knew when he left. "What if the sheriff caught you?" he asked.

"He won't." Kenny jerked his line, then let it go slack again. "You know what happened one night? Promise you won't tell mom?"

Eric thought it over. "Okay."

"The sheriff was crossing 191 when we cut him off —we didn't know it was him – and he took out after us. Man, did we fly! You never saw such smoke! You know how we lost him? The jerk slowed down for the tracks, and we got on over the hill and turned off in the cemetery. He went straight. Boy, did we laugh!"

Eric felt cold—as though the black water under the pier were lapping over his back and shoulders. It wasn't true that nothing ever changed in a small town. Sometimes things did, and you wish they hadn't.

Without betraying Kenny's trust, Eric tried to talk to his father. But dad already knew.

"Once I tried to talk to him about it. I told him I didn't ever want to catch him driving a car without a license," Mr. Weller said, polishing his heavy black shoes for church the next morning. He sighed, and the shoe dangled in his hand. "You know what he said? 'That's three years away, pop. What am I supposed to do if I can't drive?' "

Eric didn't hear a word of the sermon the following day. He didn't even hear—till his father nudged him—Pastor Dodson announce that Eric was home and ask him to stand up.

He couldn't get Kenny off his mind. He wished he could take the kid back to Washington with him, but that was asking too much of Uncle Clyde and Aunt Marie.

As they left the church, the minister shook Eric's hand. "Eric, so good to see you," he smiled, and added, "Could you drop by the house this afternoon sometime? I'd like to talk with you."

"Glad to," Eric mumbled. It ruined his plans for the day. He'd wanted to make the announcement that he was leaving on Monday. He didn't want to sit around instead, telling people how good it felt to be home.

Disgruntled, he ate Sunday dinner and went into his room to change his clothes. Kenny came in and sat down on the bed. And suddenly Eric said moodily, "Guess I should have gotten around to telling everybody sooner, but I'm going back to Washington for the summer—going to get a job there."

Kenny stared at him. "But—I thought—you just got home!"

"Well, college is coming up in the fall, and this is a chance to earn some money. My scholarship won't cover everything."

Kenny kicked swiftly at the leg of the dresser.

Eric turned around. "Hey, what's that for?"

Kenny glared at him. "So go on. Who needs you?" He got up and stalked out, banging the door hard.

Eric sighed and picked up his jacket. This wasn't his day. He'd probably make rude remarks and get the minister sore at him too. Then he'd come home and tell mom and dad he was leaving and they'd all be mad.

Pastor Dodson, however, did not want to talk about how wonderful being back was. He got right to the point. "You're the only young man around here this summer who doesn't have a job, and I'm going to ask your help," he said.

Oh, no, Eric thought. *Whatever it is, no!*

"We've got a potential problem here," the pastor went on. "There are eleven boys your brother's age in this area. And unless somebody does something for them, every one of them is headed for trouble."

He told Eric what Kenny had told him and more. Not only had some of the boys been driving cars without licenses, but some were stealing automobile parts. In fact they had a little trade going with a junk dealer in the next county.

"I'm looking for someone to run a boys' sports program this summer—baseball team, track, swimming—the works. The county is going to furnish the pay, which won't be too much, but what you'll be doing will be very important for this community. Someone's *got* to do it, Eric—and you're the only one here there is. I'll help you all I can."

Eric's Adam's apple felt as though there was a weight attached to it pulling right down to his toes. There had to be some way to get out of this gracefully—some excuse that would sound plausible. But he couldn't think of one.

"I'll give you an answer tomorrow," he said finally.

"Good," said the minister, without smiling. "We need you, Eric—I hope you won't say no."

Eric walked glumly back down the highway toward home. He could, of course, just catch the bus and go back to Washington without saying a word to the minister. Why on earth did the obligation have to fall on him? What had prompted him to come home for a brief visit instead of just staying in Washington?

He had almost reached the bend in the road when the bushes crackled behind him and Kenny came stumbling out, sobbing in high, jerky gasps.

"Kenny!"

Kenny wiped one arm across his eyes, choking back the sobs.

"We—h—had a wreck—and the car's turned over on Brigg's Lane—and R—R—Ron can't get out—"

They ran back through the birch trees toward the old county road that ran to the backwoods, and reached the place five minutes later. Another boy was sitting on the grass holding his head. Someone in the car was groaning with pain.

The car was half-overturned and had pinned Ron Butler's arm between it and the side of the ditch. The short kid on the grass was shaking with fright, but did not seem too badly hurt. Eric told him to get up and help right the car.

When they'd lifted it enough for Ray to get loose and climb out, it was easier, and when they got it upright again, Eric drove it back up on the road, its loose door banging.

"You'd better see Doc Ryder," he said to Ron,

when the boys crawled into the back seat. "Looks like that arm was mashed pretty bad."

He drove on down the highway to Ron's cousin's, where Ron had borrowed the car—past the rocky hills on each side of the road, the unpainted houses and boarded-up stores and the long stretch of dead trees, gray against a grayer sky. His heart pounded inside him, and he was dizzy with thought. He turned up a country lane and into a driveway where he stopped.

Then he faced the three boys: "I don't ever want to hear of you driving this car again," he said. "If you do, I'm going to tell the sheriff the whole story of what happened today. You got that, Ron?"

"Yes," Ron whispered.

"And something else," Eric said. "Pastor Dodson and I are starting a softball team tomorrow, and you guys are on it. You too, Ron, even if you can't play for a few weeks. I want you all at the park at ten o'clock tomorrow morning. We're going to run the legs off you guys this summer, and if you don't beat Jonesboro, we'll sell you down the river. Understand?"

Ron and the short kid nodded, their eyes wide. But Kenny's face was all grin. And somehow, as Eric and Kenny walked back home, the sky looked blue – or maybe it was pink. Eric wasn't sure. But it didn't look the way it had two days ago, and Eric almost felt good.